Sale

Speaker's Helper

Wong pg 71

THE SPEAKER'S TREASURY FOR SUNDAY SCHOOL TEACHERS

By HERBERT V. PROCHNOW

PUBLISHERS
W. A. WILDE COMPANY
BOSTON

The Speaker's Treasury for Sunday School Teachers

Library of Congress Catalog Card No. 55-10546

Made in the United States of America

PREFACE

This book is meant to be helpful to Sunday school teachers and superintendents, to ministers, and to all persons who do church school work. Many general readers may find sections of the book, such as the selections from unusual sermons, interesting and inspiring.

The first chapter explains briefly how to prepare an interesting talk and how to lead a discussion. Then there follows a wealth of practical reference material, consisting of over 1200 items, which it is believed will be of assistance to the church school worker on many occasions.

For example, Chapter II contains eighty-eight unusual stories, illustrations and selections, and Chapter III contains sixty-seven inspiring selections from inspiring sermons which the author obtained from a number of distinguished ministers. Other chapters include scores of pertinent epigrams and witticisms, hundreds of quotations from literature and the Bible classified by subject, and a number of prayers suitable for various occasions.

It is hoped that the use of this reference material will be helpful in making prepared talks and general discussions more interesting. There is much to be gained if one can illustrate a point convincingly and tell a story that inspires.

If this book is useful to those who have the great responsibility for leadership in church school work, it will have earned the place it greatly hopes to fill.

HERBERT V. PROCHNOW

CONTENTS

CHAPTER I

HOW TO PREPARE A TALK OR LEAD A DISCUSSION

Richard Chevenix Trench once said of prayer,

> "Lord, what a change within us one short hour
> Spent in Thy presence will avail to make!"

But one may also say what a great change will come into the life of a student, who is brought into His presence for one hour a week by an inspired Sunday school teacher.

The Sunday school teacher's great opportunity comes in that one hour, when he leads his class. Everything the teacher hopes to accomplish must be achieved in that single hour. The entire religious educational program is a success or a failure depending upon what takes place in that hour. How thoroughly has the teacher prepared? How well is the teaching done? How interesting is the discussion? How effectively does the teacher develop the spiritual life of each student in that one hour?

PREPARATION

No church school teacher who understands his responsibilities for leadership will ever appear before his class poorly prepared. Failure to prepare for his appearance before the class is inexcusable. When one conducts a class of twenty persons for thirty minutes, it is equal to taking 600 minutes or 10 hours of one person's time. No conscientious person would think of deliberately wasting 10 hours of one person's time. Yet, that is what occurs when a teacher fails to prepare for only one appearance before a class of twenty persons for thirty minutes. A good teacher earnestly tries to fill every class session with interesting ideas, helpful illustrations, and thoughtful questions so the students will have an enriching experience. That requires preparation. Every moment the teacher spends in thorough preparation brings benefits to the students, but even greater rewards in lasting satisfaction to the teacher for work well done. How then shall one prepare for these responsibilities?

PREPARING A TALK

Consider, first, the problem of preparing a short talk for a class. If you are to give a brief talk, there are certain definite steps which will help you to speak effectively and with clarity.

The first step in your preparation is to determine the central idea of your remarks. In conversation, you know at once what main idea you wish to convey to the listener. But when you go into a subject in more detail for five, ten, or fifteen minutes it is wise to consider exactly what you intend to say, that is, to determine the central idea of your comments. Unless you know clearly what you wish to say, you will ramble. You may even start with one idea and detour to another which is only indirectly related to the first idea. Then you may go to another idea still further from your first idea and finally wind up far from the point where you started. Failure to stick to the subject or main idea is a common error in speaking. Such a talk is uncoordinated. It is not focused on the principal idea. It leaves those who hear it confused, not knowing which idea the speaker wished to emphasize. If you do not know your subject clearly, if your mind is hazy regarding it, how can the class be expected to receive a clear idea?

Let us assume the talk deals with the parable of the Good Samaritan. The teacher may use as the central idea the enmity between the Samaritans and the Jews, as both groups claimed to be the only true inheritors of Abraham and Moses. Unless the student understands this background, he will not fully appreciate the parable. The teacher may use as the central idea the sinfulness of the enmity between the two groups and how Jesus showed men to live, by using the Samaritan as the hero. Or the teacher may use as the central idea the question the lawyer asked, "Who is my neighbor?" The question may also be reworded to read, "To Whom Can I Show Myself a Neighbor?"

After determining the central idea, it is often advisable to outline a talk as follows:

OUTLINE OF A TALK

1. Introduction
   A. In the introduction one generally states the central idea to be discussed. Using the parable of the Good Samaritan, we may state in the introduction that we shall consider the question, "Who Is My Neighbor?"
2. Main body of the talk, perhaps divided into three or four parts. In the main body of the talk we present the substance of our remarks. In the parable of the Good Samaritan we might have the following three points:
   A. What was the priest's idea of being a neighbor? Then give illustrations of how we act in similar ways today.
   B. What was the Levite's idea of being a neighbor? Then give illustrations of how we act in similar ways today.
   C. What was the Samaritan's idea of being a neighbor? Then give illustrations of how we act or might act in various situations today if we did as Jesus advised, "Go, and do thou likewise."
3. Conclusion
   In the conclusion the teacher may point out how great are the number of our neighbors in life and that everyone is our neighbor and our brother.

SOME ESSENTIALS IF YOU WISH TO SPEAK WELL

1. Know your subject thoroughly. You cannot enthuse about a subject you do not know, and therefore you cannot present it well. Enthusiasm grows out of knowledge, not out of ignorance.

2. Have your thoughts organized so they are presented in logical order.

3. Have your ideas well in mind, so that you speak fluently and straight to the point without rambling.

4. Speak clearly and sufficiently loud to be heard easily in all parts of the room.

5. Use illustrations, stories, examples, quotations, epigrams and any other tools of speech that will help you to present the lesson effectively.

LEADING A DISCUSSION

The plan for leading a discussion is essentially similar to that for preparing a talk. Under points A, B, and C in the OUTLINE OF A TALK above, the students in the class may be asked to give illustrations of similar situations in modern life. The students should also analyze what were the bad and the good points in the conduct of the three men who came upon the man who was robbed by the thieves. To what extent should one be concerned about one's immediate neighbors, and about one's neighbors in foreign countries?

If the questions and the discussion are to be most helpful, they must be related to life as the members of the class know it. Good questions stimulate discussion. A good teacher will have worked out thoughtful and stimulating questions before the class meets. Good questions on the part of the teacher will lead to questions from the students and to broad discussion.

It is important in the parable of the Good Samaritan for the student not only to discuss what was wrong in the conduct of the priest and the Levite, but also to discuss why it was wrong. When the students discuss and decide why certain conduct was wrong, it will help them to reach definite convictions by which to guide their own lives.

SOME RULES FOR WORTHWHILE DISCUSSION

1. The class must have some background material, such as personal experience, a parable from the Bible, special reading or a summary of the problem or subject to be discussed. One cannot conduct worthwhile discussion on nothing.
2. The topic for discussion should have some relationship to the real life of those in the group.
3. If the subject being discussed is a question requiring some conclusions or decisions by the group, the teacher should have prepared for her own use some of the points on both sides of the question.
4. If the discussion lags, the teacher should have suitable questions to ask to stimulate discussion.
5. If the discussion is not completed in one session, it should be completed in following meetings. No student should feel

that the discussion was simply left half completed. The teacher may say, "This is a logical place to end our discussion today. Next week we shall complete it." But the students must feel that some worthwhile part of the discussion was completed in the first session.

The class period is short, and it only comes once a week. This period should not be interrupted by persons outside the class who open the door and say, "How many are present today?" "Remind everyone to come to the picnic Friday evening." "I should like to have your offering so I can report the amount to the treasurer." This type of interruption should be eliminated.

6. The teacher and students should understand the purpose of the discussion. For example, the discussion may be to provide information; to analyze and evaluate certain problems that confront students, such as forms of entertainment; to determine what is Christian conduct under certain conditions; to decide what a Christian would do in facing certain types of civic problems. What are we trying to determine or discover in our discussion? The discussion must not be purposeless.

7. If possible, the teacher should have stories and pertinent illustrations ready for the discussion.

EFFECTIVE TOOLS FOR YOUR TALK OR DISCUSSION

After you complete a written or mental outline of the main points of your talk, or of a general discussion, you will find a number of speech tools which can be helpful to you. They will make your comments and any discussion far more interesting. These speech tools consist of such items as humorous and inspiring stories, epigrams, unusual illustrations, quotations from literature and from the Bible. There are over 1200 such items in this book.

Chapter II has eighty-eight unusual stories, illustrations and selections. A number of the stories are humorous. On many occasions, good humor may be an exceptionally helpful tool of speech in illustrating a point. Other items in Chapter II may be classified as inspiring and instructive. In your own reading you will find additional pertinent stories and illustrations. It is wise never to tell a story unless the story is definitely related to the subject and helps to emphasize or clarify an idea. No story should be used simply because it is entertaining. It must clearly help to stress a point in the lesson.

Chapter III contains many inspiring selections from inspiring sermons. Sermons were obtained by the author from a number of ministers over the United States. From these sermons, interesting and inspiring selections were chosen. These selections can be invaluable to the teacher. Some of the selections provide sufficient material for one or more entire class sessions.

Chapter IV has scores of epigrams and witticisms. Although many of these epigrams are humorous, they frequently contain terse but sage observations on various aspects of life. They help to make any discussion more colorful. Epigrams often contain in a few words an idea that might otherwise require pages to make clear. They put sparkle into discussion.

Chapter V includes hundreds of quotations from literature classified by subject. These quotations may be used to give some distinguished author's comment on the idea the class is discussing. The use of a quotation sometimes enables one to summarize a long discussion in one concise sentence.

Chapter VI contains almost 500 quotations from the Bible classified by subject. The Bible is the richest source book of quotations in the world. Many times in short talks and discussions a Biblical quotation will help to express an idea vividly.

Chapter VII contains a number of prayers suitable for various occasions. These prayers may be especially helpful to anyone who has a little difficulty in expressing himself in prayer.

In addition to the many stories, illustrations, quotations and other useful items in this book, it is suggested that the reader obtain other material from his reading and from his experiences in his daily work. For example, biographies are an especially fruitful source of inspiring stories.

Jesus often taught by parables because it was an effective way to teach. The teacher will likewise find that stories and illustrations are exceptionally valuable in emphasizing a point in a talk or discussion.

FUNDAMENTALS FOR THE TEACHER TO CONSIDER

1. Nothing can take the place of conscientious preparation by you for each class session.

2. The great objective in teaching a Sunday school class is to help the student's spiritual life and character develop into the Christian or Christ-like ideal. You may well ask, "Is my teaching helping to make Christianity an active force in the life of each of my students?"

3. Your own life and conduct, your kindness, your thoughtfulness, your fairness, your gratitude, your forgiveness—YOUR EXAMPLE—will be one of the most important lessons your students will learn.

4. Set your own class standards high by preparing for your classes to the best of your ability, and require the same high standards of the students.

5. Ask yourself as a teacher, "Why am I teaching?" "Am I giving these students my very best?"

6. Every person in your class is important. Your influence on a student's life may be far-reaching for good over many years.

7. Even if you do your best, you may sometimes be discouraged. But remember, the conscientious and careful work you do in the one hour you teach your Sunday school class each week may be the most challenging opportunity of your life. Be sure you make the most of it.

CHAPTER II

UNUSUAL STORIES, ILLUSTRATIONS AND SELECTIONS

PRAY ON THE WAY

Two boys were going to be late for Sunday School. One boy said, "Let's kneel down and pray."

The other boy who was running and out of breath said, "No, let's pray as we run to get there."

BEING A WITNESS FOR CHRIST

Do you know Jesus, someone asked a native of Africa.

"No," the native replied, "but I know a Christian missionary."

Each of us might ask himself, "How are we known to our friends and neighbors?"

THEM THAT HAS IT

The pastor said to the Southern boy, "Son, does anyone around this town enjoy religion?"

The boy replied, "Yes, sir, them that has it does."

The Southern boy was right. Those that really don't have religion can't enjoy it. Those that have it understand the joy and peace it gives.

HOW DEEP?

A young boy was brought to an orphan asylum. He was one of seven children who had all been supported by the mother. When they gave him a glass of milk, he drank a little of it and then said, "How deep shall I drink?" He had learned at home that only a part of a glass of milk was for him. Some had to be saved for the other children.

Many of us have so much of so many things. With all we have, we ought to ask, "How deep shall I drink" of my goods before I share with the less fortunate?

REMEMBER PREVIOUS JOYS

There was a dachshund once, so long
He hadn't any notion
How long it took to notify
His tail of his emotion;
And so it happened, while his eyes
Were filled with tears and sadness,
His little tail went wagging on
Because of previous gladness.

Author unknown

ALL EXCEPT ME

A Quaker is reported to have said, "Everybody is a little queer except thee and me and sometimes I fear thee is a little queer."

WISE SOCRATES

More than two thousand years ago Socrates, Athenian philosopher, said: "Could I climb the highest place in Athens, I would lift my voice and proclaim: 'Fellow citizens, why do ye turn and scrape every stone to gather wealth, and take so little care of your children, to whom one day you must relinquish it all?' "

There is no more important work in America today than that of training children. Yet the mother in the home is listed in the census as "unemployed." The teacher in the classroom usually is paid less than the worker who built the room. The teaching of the Bible, the basic book for character building, is too often forbidden in the school, and neglected in the home. The church school is understaffed, and volunteers are hard to find. » »

Fellow Americans, if we were wise, we would spend more time and more money training our children, to whom we shall soon relinquish our stores, our factories, our farms, our nation!

"I saw tomorrow marching by
  On little children's feet;
Within their forms and faces read

Her prophecy complete.
"I saw tomorrow look at me
From little children's eyes,
And thought how carefully we'd teach
If we were really wise!"

From statement by Lubbock Machine & Supply Co., Lubbock, Texas.

MONEY

The greedy search for money or success will almost always lead men to unhappiness. Why? Because that kind of life makes them depend upon things outside themselves.

Andre Maurois

BY BREAD ALONE

Man cannot live by bread alone. The making of money, the accumulation of material power, is not all there is to living. Life is something more than these, and the man who misses this truth misses the greatest joy and satisfaction that can come into his life—service for others.

Edward Bok

PRAYER

All who call on God in true faith, earnestly from the heart, will certainly be heard, and will receive what they have asked and desired.

Martin Luther

COURAGE

Dear God, give us strength to accept with serenity the things that cannot be changed. Give us courage to change the things that can and should be changed. And give us wisdom to distinguish one from the other.

Admiral Thomas C. Hart

HANDICAPS

I thank God for my handicaps, for, through them, I have found myself, my work, and my God.

Helen Keller

FAMILY

I have now disposed of all my property to my family. There is one thing more I wish I could give them, and that is the Christian religion. If they had that, and I had not given them one shilling, they would have been rich: and if they had not that, and I had given them all the world, they would be poor.

Patrick Henry

BIBLE

How many ages and generations have brooded and wept and agonized over this book! What untellable joys and ecstasies, what support to martyrs at the stake, from it! To what myriads has it been the shore and rock of safety—the refuge from driving tempest and wreck! Translated in all languages, how it has united this diverse world! Of its thousands there is not a verse, not a word, but is thick-studded with human emotion.

Walt Whitman

ACHIEVEMENT

Perseverance is a great element of success. If you only knock long enough and loud enough at the gate, you are sure to wake up somebody.

Henry Wadsworth Longfellow

Perhaps the most valuable result of all education is the ability to make yourself do the thing you have to do, when it ought to be done, whether you like it or not. It is the first lesson that ought to be learned.

Thomas H. Huxley

All growth depends upon activity. There is no development physically or intellectually without effort, and effort means work. Work is not a curse; it is the prerogative of intelligence, the only means to manhood, and the measure of civilization.

Calvin Coolidge

I desire so to conduct the affairs of this administration that if at the end, when I come to lay down the reins of power, I have lost every other friend on earth, I shall at least have one friend left, and that friend shall be down inside of me.

Abraham Lincoln

STANDARDS OF LIVING

We Americans want to live better. Although we have a high standard of living today, we plan to make it higher. But when we speak of higher standards of living, let us not limit ourselves to thoughts of common objects of convenience and comfort; for there is more to a standard of living than the material things. We need to plan for an ever-rising standard of spiritual living as well.

Admiral Ben Morell

WE DO MANY THINGS WRONG BY OURSELVES

Teacher: "And did your father help you with your arithmetic?"

Willie: "No, I got it wrong all by myself."

YOU CAN'T HIDE ANYTHING

A little boy came home from school and announced to his mother: "I'm in a fine fix at school. The teacher says I have to write more legibly, and if I do, she'll find out that I can't spell!"

WHERE LINCOLN STOOD

I am not bound to win, but I am bound to be true. I am not bound to succeed, but I am bound to live up to what light I have. I must stand with anybody that stands right, stand with him while he is right and part with him when he goes wrong.

Abraham Lincoln

BEATITUDES FOR A HOUSEWIFE

Blessed is she whose daily tasks are a labor of love, for she translates duty into privilege.

Blessed is she who mends stockings and toys and broken hearts, for her understanding is a balm to humanity.

Blessed is she who serves laughter and smiles at every meal, for she shall be blessed with goodness.

Blessed is she who preserves the sanctity of the Christian home, for hers is a sacred trust that crowns her with dignity.

Cheerful News, Eagle Rock, California

PERFECTLY CLEAR

Church Bulletin: "There will be a church picnic Thursday afternoon. If it rains in the afternoon, the picnic will be held in the morning."

IMPOSSIBLE

Never tell a young person that something cannot be done. God may have been waiting for centuries for someone ignorant enough of the impossible to do it.

Dr. J. A. Holmes

THINGS YOU NEVER REGRET

Showing kindness to an aged person. Destroying the letter written in anger. Offering the apology that saves a friendship. Stopping a scandal that is wrecking a reputation. Helping a boy find himself. Taking time to show consideration to your parents. Remembering God in all things.

The Echo

THREE THINGS

There is a wonderful mythical law of Nature that the three things we crave most in life—happiness, freedom, and peace of mind—are always attained by giving them to someone else.

General Peyton Conway March

REGENERATION

Unless there is a moral and spiritual regeneration in America, we shall all some day disappear in the dust of an atomic explosion. It is the business of the Church to bring about this regeneration.

Dwight D. Eisenhower

THE EIGHT POINTS OF LIFE

These eight points of successful living are subscribed to by many sociologists:

1. Don't contradict others, even if you know you are right.
2. Don't be inquisitive about the affairs of even your most intimate friends.
3. Don't underrate anything because you don't possess it.
4. Don't believe that everybody else in the world is happier than you.
5. Don't be rude to your inferiors in social position.
6. Don't repeat gossip, even if it does interest a crowd.
7. Learn to hide your aches and pains under a pleasant smile.
8. Learn to attend to your own business. This is especially important.

Sunshine Magazine

HER OCCUPATION

One day the census taker called and wrote down in a book, and so, as I was hanging 'round I thought I'd take a look. He had our names and ages all, and put down Dad's vocation, and after Mother's name he wrote she had "No Occupation."

Why, Mother's up before it's light, and through the work she races. She starts the breakfast, straightens things, and washes all the faces. She packs our lunches, finds our books—of course it keeps her busy—she washes, irons, sweeps, and dusts—you'd think she would be dizzy!

She bakes a cake, and maybe pies; she finds some time for sewing. There's mending, making over, too, because we all are growing. Then dinner comes, and dishes next, first one thing, then another; and when our homework bothers us, we say, "Please help us, Mother."

So, she keeps going all the time, and though she's often weary, she never gets real out of sorts—she's always gay and cheery. She keeps so busy every day, and sure needs some vacation; and yet the census man wrote down she had "No Occupation!"

Elsie Duncan Yale in
Sunshine Magazine

HAVE YOU FELT IN YOUR POCKET?

A Quaker, once hearing a person tell how much he felt for another person who was in distress and needed assistance, drily asked him, "Friend, hast thee felt in thy pocket for him?"

GOOD QUESTION

A father took his son on his knee and told him the story of the lost sheep: how it found the hole in the fence and crawled through; how glad it was to get away; how it wandered so far that it could not find its way back home. And then he told of the wolf that chased the sheep, and how, finally, the shepherd came and rescued it and carried it back to the fold.

The little boy was greatly interested, and when the story was over, he asked, "Did they nail up the hole in the fence?"

Circuit Rider

THAT DEPENDS

All day long the weary elevator operator had been patiently answering questions the department store shoppers had thrust upon him. Just before closing time a voice from the rear of the crowded car asked, "Suppose the elevator cables broke, would we go up or down?"

Unable to compose himself any longer, the operator snapped, "That, my dear lady, depends entirely on the kind of life you have led."

O'Bannon's Between Calls

THINKING OUT LOUD

A braggart is one who can't open his mouth without putting his feats into it.

When you row the other fellow across the stream, you get there yourself.

CHOICE BITS

Goodness consists not in the outward things we do, but in the inward things we are.

E. H. Chapin

Stephen Leacock, the novelist, covers the ponderous subject of luck most admirably and completely in his single-line comment: "I am a great believer in luck, and I find the harder I work the more I have of it."

NOWHERE ELSE TO GO

I have been driven many times to my knees, by the overwhelming conviction that I had nowhere else to go. . . . My own wisdom, and that of all about me, seemed insufficient for that day.

Abraham Lincoln

WILLIE'S COMPOSITION ON SOAP

Soap is a kind of stuff made into nice-looking cakes that smells good and tastes awful. Soap pieces always taste the worst when you got it into your eye. Dad says Eskimos don't never use soap. I wish I was a Eskimo.

THE COMPANY WAS GONE

Little Mabel had behaved very well while company was at her house recently. But when the guests left, mother asked Mabel to help put things away. Very soon there was a lot of noise from the linen closet.

"Stop that noise, Mabel," mother said. "What's become of your good company manners?"

"I'm putting them away with the guest towels," came the reply.

Ida B. Merrill in
Sunshine Magazine

WATER

Asked to write an essay on water, little Tommy, after chewing his pencil for a long time, wrote: "Water is a colorless liquid that turns dark when you wash in it."

THINKING OUT LOUD

It's funny how we never get too old to learn some new way to be stupid.

The road to success would have more people journeying over it if so many weren't lost trying to find short cuts.

AND THEN SOME

A prominent salesman summed up his success in three simple words—"and then some." "I discovered at an early age," he said, "that most of the differences between average and top people could be explained in three words. The top people did what was expected of them—and then some. They were thoughtful of others; they were considerate and kind—and then some. They met their obligations and responsibilities fairly and squarely—and then some. They were good friends to their friends, and could be counted on in an emergency—and then some."

Sunshine Magazine

FAILURE

Babe Ruth struck out 1,330 times. But you do not remember him for his strike-out record. You remember him for the 714 home runs which made him the home run king.

Carl Holmes

TV

The first graders were learning the letters of the alphabet. "What comes after T?" the teacher asked. One little boy quickly replied, "V."

A LONG SPEECH

Called on for an impromptu speech at a dinner one night, a Yale graduate spoke of his alma mater, and lauded her by showing that the "Y" stood for "Youth," when all might enjoy the benefits of college. "A" stood for the "appreciation" of fine things which the college makes possible. "L" for "Loyalty," the stem of all endeavor.

After about thirty minutes of that sort of thing, he arrived at and ended with the "E," which he said stood for the "Efficiency" of a Yale graduate.

Three seats down, a drowsing listener aroused himself sufficiently to murmur to his neighbor, "Thank goodness, he didn't attend the Massachusetts Institute of Technology!"

AMBITION

√ There is a loftier ambition than merely to stand high in the world. It is to stoop down and lift mankind a little higher.

Henry Van Dyke, 1852-1933

SHE LIKES HIM

It was the little girl's first day at school. The teacher asked, for the record, "What do you call your father?" "Daddy," she responded. "Yes, I know," said the teacher, "but what does your mother call him?" "Oh," said the child, "she doesn't call him anything—she likes him!"

A KIND WORD

A lonely American in a London restaurant said to the waitress, "Bring me two eggs, a cup of strong coffee and a kind word." The waitress served the food, and was turning away when the lonely man cried out, "Where's the kind word?" And she whispered, "Don't eat the eggs!"

NOT QUITE PERFECT

The plump lady stepped off the penny scales and frowned. "What's the matter, Jenny?" asked her husband. "A little overweight?"

"No, not at all," said the wife, "but according to the height table printed on the front, I ought to be six inches taller."

WASTE

After a tour of the United States, a European was being interviewed on his impressions. The man had seen our skyscrapers, inspected our factories, and visited our natural wonders. But when the reporters asked what had impressed him most, he replied simply, "The size of the American garbage can!"

HELPFUL

A young matron driving in the city, stalled her car at a traffic light. She stamped on the starter, yanked the choke, flooded the carburetor, and of course, flooded the motor.

An impatient motorist immediately behind her honked his horn incessantly.

Finally the matron driver got out, and walked back to the other car. "I'm awfully sorry, but I don't seem able to start my car," she explained. "If you'll go up there and start it for me, I'll stay here and lean on your horn for you."

The Cab Stand

GOOD TIMES

Mother was telling her small son about the good times she had when she was a little girl—riding a pony, sliding down a haystack, and wading in a brook at the farm.

"Mother," he said at last with a sigh, "I wish I'd met you earlier!"

THAT DID IT

"Why did you stop singing in the choir, Thomas?"

"Well, one Sunday, I was sick, and didn't sing, and a lot of people in the congregation asked if the noise in the organ had been fixed."

SMALL BOY'S CHRISTMAS PRAYER

"Now I lay me down to sleep, I want a train, I pray the Lord, I want a train, my soul to keep, and if I die before I wake, I want a train. Amen

Herbert V. Prochnow

GLAD TO MEET YOU

Billie Burke was enjoying a trans-Atlantic ocean trip when she noticed that a gentleman at the next table was suffering from a bad cold.

"Uncomfortable?" she asked sympathetically.

The man nodded.

"I'll tell you what to do for it," she offered. "Go back to your stateroom, and drink a lot of orange juice. Take two aspirin tablets. Cover yourself with all the blankets you can find. Sweat the cold out. I know what I'm talking about. I'm Billie Burke of Hollywood."

The man smiled warmly, and said,
"Thanks. I'm Dr. Mayo, of the Mayo Clinic."

RAISING THE BUDGET

Who says artists aren't practical people? From an art department we've learned about a well-known Massachusetts painter who was solicited by his church for a donation.

"I haven't any money," said the artist, "but I'll give a $200 picture."

But when all contributions were in, there was still a budget deficit, and the minister asked the congregation to increase the donations.

"All right," said the artist, "I'll do my share. I'll raise the price of the picture to $300."

PLEASE REMIT

A farmer wrote to a mail order house as follows: "Please send me one of those gasoline engines you show on page 785, and if it's any good I'll send you a check for it."

He received the following reply from the firm: "Please send us the check, and if it's any good we'll send you the engine."

POLITENESS

"How did you happen to hit the pedestrian?" the policeman asked.

"But I didn't hit him," declared the motorist. "I came to the stop sign and stopped. I motioned to him to go across, and he fainted!"

A SPLENDID FAMILY

The father of Success is Work. The mother of Success is Ambition.

The oldest son is Common Sense. Some of the other boys are: Perseverance, Honesty, Thoroughness, Foresight, Enthusiasm, and Cooperation.

The oldest daughter is Character. Some of the other sisters are: Cheerfulness, Loyalty, Courtesy, Care, Economy, Sincerity, and Harmony.

The baby of the family is Opportunity.

Get acquainted with "father" and you will be able to get along real well with the rest of the family.

SEVEN "MINDS"

Mind your tongue. Don't let it speak hasty, cruel, unkind, or wicked words.

Mind your eyes. Don't permit them to look on bad books, pictures, or objects.

Mind your ears. Don't suffer them to listen to wicked speeches, songs, or words.

Mind your lips. Don't let the food of gluttony enter between them.

Mind your hands. Don't let them steal or fight, or write any evil words.

Mind your feet. Don't let them walk in the steps of bad people.

Mind your heart. Don't let anything but good get into your heart—to think good, to do good, to love good.

Sunshine Magazine

THREE WONDERFUL WORDS

What are the three most wonderful words?

The single man said that in his estimation, the three words were, "I love you."

The second man, happily married, argued that "Home, sweet home," were the words.

The third man then spoke. He was a business man, and his vote was for the words, "Enclosed find check."

HAPPY ENDING

He had taken his youngest son to the pet shop to pick out a puppy as a birthday present and the lad spent half an hour looking over the assortment of dogs in the window.

"Decided which one you want?" asked his father.

"Yes," replied the boy, pointing to one puppy which was enthusiastically wagging his tail. "The one with the happy ending."

EXAMPLE

While Calvin Coolidge was President, a display of social nicety took place in the White House one morning. The Ambassador from France was breakfasting with the President, and discussing an important matter. He was somewhat taken aback when Mr. Coolidge poured his cup of milk into a saucer. A gentleman to the last, the French Ambassador did the same thing with his milk.

The President smiled slightly, said nothing, but stooped down and gave his saucer to a gray cat waiting at his feet.

TOUGH AT HOME, TOO

A lady was entertaining her friend's small son. "Are you sure you can cut your meat?" she asked, after watching his struggles.

"Oh, yes," he replied, without looking up from his plate. "We often have it as tough as this at home."

COURTESY

She was an exasperating customer and hadn't bought a thing.

"Why is it," she snapped at last, "that I never get what I ask for in your store?"

"Perhaps, madam," said the assistant, "it's because we are too polite."

GOD IS LOVE

Once while riding in the country, I saw on a farmer's barn a weather vane on the arrow of which was inscribed the words: "God Is Love."

I turned in at the gate and asked the farmer, "What do you mean by that? Do you think God's love is changeable; that it veers about as that arrow turns in the winds?"

"Oh, no!" cried the farmer, "I mean that whichever way the wind blows, God is still love."

Chas. Spurgeon

THE NAME ISN'T IMPORTANT

It is said that Lincoln once said to an argumentative group, "How many legs would a sheep have if you called his tail a leg?" The group answered promptly, "Five." "Wrong," said Lincoln, it would have only four. Calling the tail a leg would not make it so."

There is no doubt that the unbeliever wishes to call sin by every other name but sin, but that does not change its essential character in the sight of God.

ON THE GLOWING WESTERN SLOPES

The records are full of cases of folks who have stayed gingery and productive, even into the 80's and 90's.

Michelangelo painted the ceiling of the Sistine Chapel on his back on a scaffold at near 90.

George Santayana said at 82, "I have never been happier in my life than right now."

Daniel Auber wrote his "Dream of Love" in his 80's, and said, "I'm not 80; I am four times 20."

Paderewski at 79 played the piano superbly.

At 88 John Wesley preached every day.

Tennyson published "Crossing the Bar" at 83.

Booth Tarkington wrote sixteen novels after 60—some of them when he was almost totally blind.

Of Benjamin Franklin, Walter B. Pitkin said: "Men have forgotten the first half of his life. The world will never forget the second." Franklin went to France in the service of his country at 78, and wrote his autobiography at over 80.

Sunshine Magazine

FOLLOW INSTRUCTIONS

Teacher (to tardy boy): "Why are you so late?"

Boy: "Well, I always obey the laws."

Teacher: "Well, just what do you mean?"

Boy: "There's a sign down the road that says, 'school ahead, go slow.'"

HARD JOB

After directing research in American industry for years and developing many important inventions, Charles F. Kettering commented that a message can be sent around the world in a seventh of a second, but it may take years to force a single idea through a quarter inch of human skull.

BOTH KNEES NEEDED

A lecturer recently declared at the outset of his message that he "received his moral training at the knee of a devout mother and across the knee of a determined father." One wonders how many of the oncoming generation will be able to make such a statement.

Union Church News,
Lima, Peru

NEXT THE MILLENNIUM

The John Deere house magazine, *The Connecting Link,* reports that a husband in St. Louis, Mo., recently inserted this "To Whom It May Concern" public notice in a local newspaper:

"I *am* responsible for all debts and obligations of my wife, and am more than happy to be the provider for the woman who has made the past 21 years of lovingkindness the nicest years of my life."

INDIVIDUAL LIBERTY

From the moment that Christ held up the idea that prince and peasant alike were in the image of God, and could think God's thoughts in the form of arts, sciences, tools, and laws, all mankind began a great upward march. The fetters were struck from all men. With this idea of individual liberty man found himself. He set forth upon the long journey upward to freedom. Each person is the lord of his own life, and, in the words of St. Paul, "Every man shall give an account of himself unto God."

HER "ENEMIES"

Seven-year-old Ellen was punished one night by not being allowed to dine at the big table with the rest of the family. Instead, she was made to eat her dinner alone at a little table in the corner of the dining room. The rest of the family set about ignoring her completely until they heard her saying grace over her solitary supper in these words: "I thank Thee, Lord, for preparing a table before me in the presence of mine enemies."

FAME

But yesterday the word of Caesar might
Have stood against the world; now dies he there,
And none so poor to do him reverence.

Shakespeare, Julius Caesar, III-2

HE KNEW HIS DAD

After careful thought, a school teacher decided to give full credit to a pupil for his answer to an arithmetic problem.

The question: "If your father sold fifteen hundred bushels of grain for $2 per bushel, what would he get?"

The answer: "A new car."

A CHARACTER QUIZ

1. If you found a pocketbook with $1,000, would you give it to the owner if no one would ever know you found it?"
2. If you could advance yourself by unfair methods, would you do it if no one would ever find out you were unfair?
3. If the bus driver failed to collect your fare, would you voluntarily pay it?
4. If there were no locks on any house, store, or bank, would you take anything if no one would ever find out?
5. If your business partner died, would you pay his relatives their fair share, if you did not have to pay them?
6. If you were an employer trying to hire an efficient, honest, and competent employee, would you hire yourself at your salary?
7. If you are an employer would you like to be working for yourself with the wages, hours, and working conditions you provide?
8. If you are a parent, would you like to be the child of a parent just like you are?

9. If you had your choice, would you like to live in a community with people working in church, civic and community affairs just like you do?

10. If you had to live with someone just like you are for the rest of your life, would you look forward to it as a wonderful opportunity and privilege?

Herbert V. Prochnow
in Sunshine Magazine

ALONG THE WAY

Roy H. Stetler, a successful publisher of Harrisburg, Pennsylvania, bought a new car. This is what he said editorially concerning it:

"When our new car was delivered, I could not resist taking a little spin along the river. I found myself thinking about the affair. So, as is my habit in matters of this sort, I started to talk to God about the new car. Don't know why, but I had never before discussed our other new cars with God. As I recall, I was led to say something like this: 'God, we are grateful to you for this new car. Because you made it possible for us to have it, we should like to dedicate it to you. First, we want you to go with us, for we feel we are likely to drive better if we know you are one of our riders. Then, we don't want to drive anywhere that would be objectionable to you. We want to go where you direct, and in no direction where you would have to leave us to ourselves.'

"Does such a prayer sound silly? It occurs to me that if more cars were thus dedicated, there might be fewer accidents. If the 'cattle upon a thousand hills' are His, I am sure the automobiles on the thousands of highways are His too."

Sunshine Magazine

GOOD QUESTION

A small boy visiting New York City went up in the elevator to the top of the Empire State Building. As he passed the sixty-fifth floor, he gulped, turned to his father, and said, "Daddy, does God know we are coming?"

HER MINISTER

The six-year-old daughter of a clergyman was sick and was put to bed early. As her mother was about to leave, she called her back. "Mommy, I want to see my daddy."

"No, dear," her mother replied," your daddy is busy and must not be disturbed."

"But, Mommy," the child persisted, "I want to see my daddy."

The mother again replied, "No, your daddy must not be disturbed."

But the little one came back with even more determination.

"Mommy," she declared, "I am a sick woman, and I want to see my minister."

GIVING

We all know about the preacher who said that "It takes three books to run a church—a hymn book, a prayer book, and a pocket book." However, the latter "book," so many feel, is just a man-added nuisance. Is it?

No, the giving of money is not a man-made rule at all. It is born in the heart of our God. And if I know that I have been forgiven much, how can I give except in the measure of "much"? I say that I "love" God. Love is giving. God also "loved," and He gave that of which He only had one—His only begotten son. Christ "loved me and gave Himself for me." When we say we love God, then it ought to be more than just lip service. Love dare not stop at the edge of the pocket. It must open the pocketbook, and let the surrendered heart dictate the terms of giving. Our Lord said: "Give."

R. R. Belter

LOVE YOUR ENEMIES

There is such a destructive reflex action in the soul of a man who allows himself to hate another that it is surprising any sensible person would allow himself to be subjected to it. Hate is a poison which vitiates all character, and brings about the degeneration of personality.

This story was told of General Robert E. Lee: Hearing

General Lee speak in the highest terms to President Davis about a certain officer, another officer, greatly astonished, said to him, "General, do you not know that the man of whom you speak so highly to the President is one of your bitterest enemies, and misses no opportunity to malign you?"

"Yes," replied General Lee, "but the President asked my opinion of him; he did not ask for his opinion of me."

Sunshine Magazine

NOT EASY TO UNDERSTAND

Little Margery had been watching a fasionable wedding from outside the church. Returning home, she reported: "Well, I can't make out whom she married. She went in with an old man, and when she came out she was with a different man altogether."

THINKING OF ONE'S SELF

Two very young boys climbed on a small hobbyhorse. After a few minutes, one said to the other, "If one of us got off, I could ride better."

GREAT OCCASIONS

Great occasions do not make heroes or cowards; they simply unveil them to the eyes of men. Silently or imperceptibly, as we wake or sleep, we grow strong or we grow weak, and at last some crisis shows us what we have become.

Bishop Westcott

TAKE ANOTHER LOOK

A big-league umpire once remarked that he could never understand how crowds in the grandstand, hundreds of feet from the plate, could see better and judge more accurately than he, when he was only seven feet away.

Another man commented that in life, too, we call strikes on a chap when we are too far away to understand. Perhaps, if we had a closer view of the man and his problems, we would reverse our decisions.

Friendly Thoughts

WONDER-WORKING POWER

All of us hunger for a word of praise.

Mark Twain is credited with saying that "I can live for two months on a good compliment."

Every normal person secretly yearns to be recognized and appreciated. It is a human trait common to all of us. Whenever we recognize a good deed, a job well done, or a thoughtful act of our fellowman, and show our appreciation by a word of praise, the life of each is made a little happier and richer.

When properly used, honest and sincere praise possesses wonder-working powers:

It helps to win and hold friends.
It stimulates interest and enthusiasm.
It encourages cooperation and efficiency.
It promotes happiness and good fellowship.
It increases self-confidence and loyalty.
It stimulates a feeling of importance and self-respect.
It is a remedy for some of the ills and discouragements of life.

J. B. Shores, in Between Ourselves
from Sunshine Magazine

Kindness

CHAPTER III

INSPIRING SELECTIONS FROM INSPIRING SERMONS

WHAT IS SUCCESS?

The desire to be successful people is common to us all. No one likes to feel that he is a failure. Several years ago I raised the question in my own mind, "What is success anyway?" In an effort to find an answer I wrote letters to sixty prominent American citizens asking for a definition and suggested that they define success in a single sentence. I received forty-eight replies. Letters came from such persons as Christopher Morley, Clare Booth Luce, Charles Mayo, Sumner Welles, Alfred Sloane, Harold Stassen, Eleanor Roosevelt, Henry Kaiser and others. You can imagine these letters made interesting reading. The one I liked most of all was that submitted by Dr. Kenneth Scott Latourette, professor of Oriental History at Yale University, who simply wrote and said, "I know of no better description of a successful person than that found in the words of our Lord, "For whosoever shall save his life shall lose it but whosoever shall lose his life for My sake and the Gospel's, the same shall find it."

C. C. Meeden

LOOKING AHEAD

Dr. Paul Lamont Thompson, a former president of Shurtleff College, spoke in chapel one day and used this statement as his text, "Young man, there is an old man ahead of you. It is you." What you will eventually be you are now becoming. Make no mistake about that.

C. C. Meeden

BUILDING THE TEMPLE OF GOD

The Jews have a beautiful legend about the building of the Temple. On the Temple site two brothers had adjoining farms. One brother was married and had children; the other brother had no wife or children. When the harvest time came around the brother who was married and had children said to himself, "My brother over yonder has no wife or children, and lives a lonely life. I will cheer his heart by taking some of my sheaves and adding to his harvest." Thus it was that each morning each brother's stack of sheaves rose higher, and both brothers wondered how it happened. At length the mystery was solved. One night, as the harvest moon was shining, the two brothers met one another, each with his arms full of sheaves and bound for his brother's field. There where they met one another that night, according to the legend, rose the temple of God.

Clarence Edward Macartney

A BETTER BOY

A small boy had been in trouble all day. In the morning he had broken a neighbor's window while playing baseball. At the lunch table he had quarreled with his little sister and made her cry. That afternoon he had broken his promise not to tease the canary. Exasperated, his mother told him he must go to bed without his dinner. Before he crawled into bed, she suggested that he include in his prayers a plea that God would make him a better boy. As he knelt by the side of the bed, his mother was astounded to hear him say: "Dear God, please make me a better boy if you can; but if you can't, never mind, 'cause I'm having an awful good time like I am!"

Parents who are prepared are equal to any emergency. They have learned how important it is to treat the child as an individual with feelings and yearnings too, so that they as parents are able to pause a minute, remembering their own childhood, and putting themselves in the shoes of their child.

Robert E. Edgar

THE THINGS YOU REMEMBER

It's queer the things you remember when life has crumbled suddenly and left you standing alone. It's not the big important things, nor the plans of years, nor the hopes you've worked on so hard. It's the little things you hadn't noticed at the time—

the way a hand touched yours and you were too busy to notice, the hopeful inflection of a voice you really didn't bother to listen to. John Carmichael found that out. All he could remember now was that his little girl had said something one evening, perhaps three weeks ago.

That particular evening he had brought home from the office the finished draft of the stockholders' report. Things being as they were the report meant a great deal. He had to be sure it was right. Just as he turned a page, Marge, his little daughter, came with a book under her arm and said, "Look, Daddy"; he looked briefly. "New book, eh?" "Yes, Daddy, will you read me a story in it?" "No, dear, not just now," he said. Marge stood there and he read through a paragraph telling the stockholders about certain replacements of machinery at the factory, and Marge's voice with a timid, hopeful little inflection was saying: "But Mommy said you would, Daddy." He looked over the top of his typed script; "I'm sorry, Marge, maybe Mommy will read to you; I'm busy now, dear." "No," Marge said politely, "Mommy is much busier upstairs. Isn't this a lovely picture?" "Oh yes, beautiful," he said, "but I have to work tonight; some other time, Marge."

Marge stood there with the book open at the picture. It was a long time before she said anything else. He read through two more pages explaining in full detail the shift of the market in the past twelve months, the plans outlined for the sales department in meeting these problems and the advertising program which had been devised to increase the demand for the product. "But it's a lovely picture, Daddy; this story looks so exciting," Marge said. "I know," he said, "some other time. Now just run along." "Read some other time, Daddy?" "Of course," he said, "sure, you bet!" She put the book down on the stool at his feet and said, "Well, whenever you get ready just read it to yourself, only read it loud enough so I can hear it too." "Sure," he said, "sure, later." And that was what John Carmichael was remembering now—the well-mannered child had touched his hand with timid fingers and said, "read it loud enough so I can hear too." That was why he now put his hand on the book and took it from the table where he had piled some of Marge's things, picking them up from the floor where she had left them, and opened it to this lovely picture.

Reading the story his lips moved stiffly with anguish to form the words. He didn't try to think any more, and for a little while he even forgot the horror and the bitterness of his hate for the half drunken driver who had careened down the street in a second-hand car and who was now in jail on manslaughter charges. He didn't even see his wife, white and silent, dressed for Marge's funeral, standing in the doorway trying to make her voice say calmly, "I'm ready, dear. We must go." He didn't see or hear any of this because John Carmichael was reading: "Once upon a time there was a little girl who lived in a woodcutters' hut in the black forest, and she was so fair that the birds forgot their singing looking at her." And then there came a day when he was reading it to himself, but loud enough for her to hear too, just perhaps.

Robert E. Edgar

DEFEAT AND TRIUMPH

Jesus taught us to use defeat. Most of us are defeated from time to time in what we undertake. One hundred men start a business tomorrow and only a few are in business six years from now. We start a million children in school, but at the end of ten or twelve years only a small percent are still in the educational process. Defeated! We long to be well and set ourselves for health, but along comes an illness or an accident and we are defeated.

George Washington hardly won a battle in the Revolutionary War but he studied the situation, withdrew, conserved his reserves, and out of one defeat after another, won the war. Mark Twain, in a financial deal, lost everything he had. But instead of sitting down and nursing his defeat, it spurred him on and he came back to pay every debt and thus use his defeat. Admiral Byrd was twice dropped from the United States Navy for physical defects, but he flew to the North Pole and he flew to the South Pole and was made an Admiral in the Navy which had twice dropped him.

The wedding service reads, "I, John, take thee, Mary, to be

my wedded wife, and I do promise and covenant before God and these witnesses to be thy loving and faithful husband in plenty and in want, in joy and in sorrow, in sickness and in health as long as we both shall live." Then she says the same. Life is like that. There is want, sorrow, and sickness. There is defeat for everyone somewhere along the line. What shall we do about it? Jesus teaches us that we must not waste even defeat. We must use it.

Peter vowed that he would never deny Jesus, but he did, three times! Yet in every list of Disciples, Peter is first. Jesus taught Peter that the only failure is within. "I have prayed for thee that thy faith fail not." All the temptations and sins of the world cannot ruin a life until they get inside, until we consent to them. Fortunate circumstances do not make life victorious, but often unhappy. Yet Jesus, poor, rejected of man, was a victor through defeat. Epictetus, a slave and crippled, Robert Louis Stevenson, Helen Keller, were victors through defeat. The spiritual enrichment of mankind has come not from men who succeeded outwardly but from men and women, defeated in this and that, yet who have won a great spiritual victory within.

Phillips Brooks once received a letter reading as follows: "I'm a tailor in a little shop near your church. When I can, I attend. When I hear you preach I forget you, for you make me think of God." Phillips Brooks tried to be a teacher at Harvard and was defeated. Yet he became the greatest preacher in the America of his day. Paul wanted to go to preach in Asia, but he was not permitted and he felt defeated. Yet he turned to Europe and so today we have Christianity because Paul did not waste this defeat in his plans. David Livingstone wanted to go to China, but this plan was broken. He went to Africa and there became, I suppose, the world's best loved missionary.

Do not throw away your pain. Use it! Do not throw away your defeat. Save others and so save yourself! Do not throw away defeat. Bring something greater out of it! When the fight begins within, a man's worth something. Gather up the broken pieces that nothing be lost.

J. Walter Malone

A CO-WORKER WITH GOD

Rufus Jones, that wise, whimsical, great hearted Quaker teacher who died a few years ago, was fond of telling the story of a man who took a very rough and tough plot of land and after years of struggle with stumps, and rocks, and weeds and bushes made a wonderful vegetable garden out of it. He and Dr. Jones stood looking at it. The man was pretty proud, even to the point of boastfulness. "I did this. I did that." "You must remember," said Dr. Jones, "that you had help." "I did it alone," said the man. "No," said Jones, "you and God did it together. Surely He helped grow these wonderful tomatoes and beans." "Yes," said the man, "I suppose He did. But you should have seen how it looked when God had it alone. It was a wilderness!"

This, then, is the first obvious wilderness: our world "as God made it"; or, if you prefer, the world as man finds it. And the voice that cries out of that wilderness is the inner voice which urges man to shape that given world nearer to his own heart's desires. We have inherited from the prodigal hand of God the raw stuff of the planet, and voices have cried to us in all ages that we, as well as He, can have a hand in shaping it. He made the world? Yes. But we can make the world less wild and more fair, less full of hunger and more full of food, less full of pain and death, more full of healing and life.

Boynton Merrill

GIVING LIFE AWAY

The idea of finding life by losing ourselves in order to enrich others is demonstrated in many areas of life. You will find it, for example, in the field of science. Dr. Alfred Blalock, of Johns Hopkins, gives himself to heart surgery and blue babies have a chance to live. Madame Curie gives herself to the search for pure radium and hope blossoms again for the victims of cancer. Edward Jenner gives himself to the study of vaccine and the world is delivered from the scourge of smallpox. Alexander Graham Bell gives himself to a study of vibrations and people converse over a gadget called the telephone. George

Washington Carver gives himself to the little peanut and asked God to unfold to him its secrets, and from it there comes forth a score of products to bless mankind. . . .

In the field of religion the same principle applies. The Apostle Paul gives himself to the Gospel of Jesus Christ and looses the power that delivers Caesar from the throne. Wycliffe gives himself to a study of the original languages of the Bible and becomes the "Morning Star of the Reformation." Luther gives himself to the doctrine of justification by faith and starts the 16th Century Revolution. Albert Schweitzer, great man of medicine and music, goes as a missionary to Africa and spends his life battling against white ants and the superstitions of black men and becomes a miracle missionary of this generation.

C. C. Meeden

THE STUBBORN CHRIST

Jesus comes to the final crisis. It is the cross. How easy to summon men to sacrifice! He stands before Pilate. Did He ask Himself, "Why not explain it to him? He appears to be a reasonable man. He has said, 'I find no fault in this man.' Would it not be possible through a nod of the head, an expression upon the face, to make it clear to Pilate that I desire to talk to him alone? It could be explained so easily. I could promise to preach no more. I could tell him that I understand his problems. He is a governor. There must be no disturbance. The common people have heard me, but law and order must be maintained." And of course it would be so happy to return to Nazareth and live again the precious hours with his Mother, to visit the synagogue once in a while, to climb the far away mountains, and to be alone in meditation. Why not do this? But, no. He had made a decision in the Garden. "Not my will but thine be done." If it were necessary that one's death reveal a love that gives itself that others may know its meaning, then that must be done. In silence, he stands before his accusers. He does not give full answer to the man who holds his life in his hands. At the time, he utters a brief answer that well nigh condemns Him. The judge asks, "Art thou a king?" He replied, "Thou hast said." He is perfectly human in this crisis.

A terrible cry is heard, "My God, why hast thou forsaken me?" But master of crisis, as well as master of men, He offers the eternal prayer, "Father forgive them, for they know not what they do." He becomes the world's Suffering Servant, and more, the world's Saviour, God's Son.

G. Bromley Oxnam

WHAT DID YOU MAKE OF IT

The marked difference between men is determined by how they face life, what they make of it. Studdert Kennedy expresses his deep concern regarding the Judgment Day, feeling that God's primary question will be, "Well, what did you make of it?" As you observe life around you, you are very sure that the results are determined not by the presence or absence of difficulty, but by the manner in which difficulty has been faced.

Edmund Vance Cook, in his poem, "How Did You Die?", concludes each of three stanzas in this manner: "It isn't the fact that you're hurt that counts, but only, how did you take it?"; "It isn't the fact that you're licked that counts—it's how did you fight and why?"; "It isn't the fact that you're dead that counts, but only—how did you die?"

Milton A. Marcy

A RESPECTABLE SINNER

A minister was conducting a funeral service for one of his members. During the eulogy he leaned over and remarked, "This corpse has been a member of our church for twenty years." Another minister in a similar situation said during the eulogy, "Our brother was not what you would call a good man. He is what we would call a respectable sinner." A man or a church are Christian only when they live above the law, do more than is required to live a clean, decent and respectable life. The church and its people must go the second mile in their generosity, their loyalty, their love, and their devotion.

John Homer Miller

MAN AT HIS BEST

The colored slaves set free in '61-'65 must have been an anchorless, unhappy lot. Carl Elmore tells a story of how one of them must have been lifted out of his deplorable state by a superb act of Christian courtesy offered by a gentleman who instinctively did the noble thing.

It was in one of the most aristocratic churches of Richmond, Virginia, soon after the Civil War. The rector had just invited the congregation to come forward to kneel at the altar rail to receive Holy Communion. Suddenly almost a gasp of dismay ran through the pews for, down the aisle, alone, came an elderly Negro, an ex-slave, from his seat in the remote rear. He climbed the chancel steps and knelt, but no one stirred. To break bread, even the bread of Christ, with colored ex-slaves simply was "not done." No one moved. Then a whitehaired gentleman, obviously beautifully bred, sensed suddenly what was happening. He rose, walked down the aisle, went up the chancel steps and knelt beside the kneeling Negro. It was General Robert E. Lee.

Boynton Merrill

HOW TO REPAY KINDNESS

Dwight L. Moody on a certain occasion had shown great kindness to a friend. In thanking him, the friend said that he hoped one day that he would be able to repay the kindness to Moody. In his quick, abrupt way, Moody answered: "Don't wait for me! Do it to the first person who comes along!"

Clarence Edward Macartney

CHANGING HUMAN NATURE

There is an old cliche which says, "You can't change human nature." Students of the Bible have added a second phrase which is now almost as common—"But God can."

Philip F. McNairy

IN THE PRESENCE OF GOD

The real reason why we ought to be in Church is for the worship of Almighty God. The best thing that can happen is not that you should hear an inspiring sermon or enjoy wonderful music, but that you should have the sense that you have been ushered into the very presence of God. We are always in the presence of God every waking moment of our lives, but when we are in church we want to become consciously aware of that presence. We are to give ourselves to the adoring recognition that we are in the presence of the Worshipful. When we give ourselves to this we are really engaging in what has been called "the supreme act of a man's life."

Albert J. Penner

BE NOT QUICK TO JUDGE

How often we wrongly judge another because we do not really know him. John Wesley in his "Journal" confesses how wrongly he once judged a man who he thought was extremely stingy. It seemed to Wesley that this man had a reasonably good income and yet he lived like a miser. One day Wesley harshly took this man to task. And then he learned to his chagrin and embarrassment that this man was denying himself and indeed living on a few poor vegetables, mostly turnips, in order that he might rid himself of a debt of long standing.

Many a person is bearing a load of which we know nothing, and we should not be too quick to judge. Rather should we be quick to judge ourselves.

To refrain from judging others is a negative virtue. To show kindness and compassion is positive. All of us bear certain burdens, and many bear heavier burdens than we know. If all hearts were open and all desires known to us as they are known to God, what tears and heartaches and sufferings would be disclosed.

Albert J. Penner

A CHRISTIAN LIFE

Everyone can speak the language of the Christian life. You do not have to be ordained. You do not need to be a graduate from a theological seminary, or a college. You do not have to be a religious worker. You do not need a pulpit to preach from or a newspaper to express your views.

You can speak the language of the Christian life on a crowded bus. As a matter of fact, people often unconsciously reveal themselves in the midst of crowds. Angers flare, meanness and selfishness are revealed. So also is good temper, patience, magnanimity and good will. You can speak that language in your office, in the school room, at directors' meetings, at the party or the club.

Albert J. Penner

WILLING TO BE FORGOTTEN

A gifted young man upon graduation from one of our well-known colleges offered himself as a missionary for service in Africa. There were those who protested. They felt he was throwing his life away and burying his great talents in the ground. To one of these protesting friends he spoke in these words: "In the building of a bridge, before the great span can be thrown across the river, one must first build a foundation. For this, immense boulders are dumped into the water. Most of them are submerged and utterly forgotten. But without them no bridge could be built. I am willing to be such a boulder, submerged and forgotten, if upon me can rest a span that will be part of a bridge of understanding and friendship between my country and Africa."

"I am willing to be submerged and forgotten,"—that is not the way the natural man speaks. He says, like the builders of Babel, "Come let us build us a city and tower . . . and let us make us a name." He says, "I want to get rich, I want to be successful, I want to be famous, I want . . . I, I, I." He may not say so in so many words but what he means is: "I think of myself first. I think of myself last. I think of myself all the time."

Albert J. Penner

CARELESS WORDS

How great a forest is set on fire by a little spark! Some unthinking person drops a cigarette among the pine needles and a whole mountainside is burned over, remaining disfigured and blackened for a long period of time. Some unthinking person drops careless words, and men are ruined, friendships are broken, churches are destroyed. May God set a watch upon our lips!

Sidney W. Powell

NO DUTIES

Phillips Brooks, returning from a trip to the Far East, was asked about what articles he had brought back with him and what customs duty he had to pay. The friend, facetiously, asked him too if he had tried to bring back a new religion. Brooks replied that he had not tried to do so; but if he had done so, there would have been no difficulty about customs duties, for America would be glad to import a religion "without any duties."

Clarence Edward Macartney

WHAT VALUE HAVE CONQUESTS?

When Napoleon was marching from victory to victory in Europe, we are told that his aged mother kept asking over and over again, "Will it last? Will it last?" The answer to that question was given at Waterloo. It was written at St. Helena where Napoleon, during his exile at Longwood, wrote these words: "You speak of conquerors; but of what value are our conquests? Alexander, Caesar, Charlemagne, and I have founded empires. But on what? On force! Jesus alone founded his empire on love, and, at this hour, millions of men would die for him. I inspired multitudes . . . but now that I am here at St. Helena, chained to this rock, who fights and wins empires for me? What an abyss between my deep misery and the eternal reign of Christ! He is everywhere proclaimed, loved, and adored, and his sway is extending over all the earth."

Clarence W. Cranford

ENCOURAGING EVIL

The church member who neglects the house of worship and prayer is a comfort and encouragement to those who never go. If a Christian man's speech is just as worldly and profane as a man of the world, then he is a comfort to worldly men. If a woman who is a Christian is just as much of a busybody and gossip and talebearer as the unbelieving woman who lives next to her, she is a comfort and an encouragement to those who do evil. If a Christian man in his business dealings is harder and sharper than an unbeliever, or if he deviates from the course of honor and rectitude and honesty, he is a comfort to all who deal dishonestly and unfairly. If a Christian man laughs just as heartily as a worldly man at a salacious or irreverent anecdote, he comforts all who talk that way. If a Christian man is silent when Christ and his cause and his Church are evil spoken of, his silence encourages all those who are against Christ and His Church.

If a Christian man delights to hear and take up an evil report against his neighbor, then he helps the ungodly and is a helper of the calumniator and the slanderer. If a Christian man when he is wronged is just as bitter and harsh and unforgiving as the non-Christian man, then he is an encouragement to all who despise the spirit of Jesus. In one of his passages where he rebukes members of the church at Corinth for bitter and unbrotherly conduct, Paul says, "Are ye not worldly?" that is, "Are ye not behaving just as the unbelievers, the pagans, do?" That is the point. The Christian man confesses to a higher standing. He has committed himself to a different way of life than the world, and for him to depart from that way is not only a sin for him personally, but it encourages other men to do evil.

Clarence Edward Macartney

YOUR LIFE DOES COUNT

On one occasion a prominent astronomer was lecturing on the newest finds of his science. He unfolded the amazing discoveries being made concerning the extent and operation of our universe. After he had finished, he threw the meeting open for questions. One person asked, "Professor, after all you have told us about the complexity of our universe, do you think that a God great enough to make such a world could be concerned about us mortals?" The professor paused thoughtfully, and replied, "It depends on how great your God is!"

That's exactly it. Our Christian faith affirms that God is great enough to know you, the creature He has made, great enough to care about you personally. . . .

The supreme claim of our faith is this: you are so important to God that He has given His Son for you.

In God's eyes, you are not just one member of a mass; you are a person whom He knows, whom He loves. Your highest good in this present life is a matter of great concern to Him. He wills your deepest joy; and you can find joy only in His will. Your destiny is of the utmost importance to Him; He gave Himself in order to help you achieve eternal fellowship with Him.

Don't you ever say to yourself again that you do not matter, that you are of no importance. You are one for whom Christ died! You ought never to think of yourself as a mere nobody, so long as God thinks that much of you.

Chester A. Pennington

THE CATCHIN' KIND OF RELIGION

A rough and ready preacher in Iowa preached recently on the subject, "What Kind of Religion Do You Have?" I think he meant, "Do You Have Reality in Your Religion?", because his three points were as follows: (1) Do you have religion? (2) Do you have the catchin' kind? (3) How many have caught it from you?

A great faith in God, a quality of goodness in our personal and social relations with others, the touch of heroism in our personal living, will make religion real not only to ourselves but to those who know us.

J. Walter Malone

"LAUNCH OUT INTO THE DEEP AND LET DOWN YOUR NETS"

Peter, with James and John, the sons of Zebedee, had fished the night through, dragging heavy nets through the cool waters of Galilee. Luke records that they "had toiled all night and taken nothing." Now they were washing their nets on the sandy shore. They were not in the best of good humor when Jesus, followed by a crowd, asked if he might use one of their ships for a pulpit. When he had finished preaching, he turned smiling to Simon Peter and said, "Launch out into the deep and let down your nets." Peter's answer is revealing: "Master, we have toiled all night and taken nothing; nevertheless, at thy word I will let down the nets." When the nets came up, they were filled with "a multitude of fish."

Every time I read that story it stimulates my imagination. Whether Luke meant it as a parable, I do not know, but it seems like a portrait of our own experience. We toil all night with the issues of life and often take nothing. Sleepless and restless we wrestle with problems, trying to decide difficult alternatives, and the dawn finds us precisely where we were at dusk, on the fence. When we are honest with ourselves, we know we have been struggling mostly in the shallows, leaving God out of our calculations. Preoccupied with ourselves, our wants, our desires, our feelings, our angers, it has not occurred to us to "launch out into the deep" where God calls us to consider his will and his way. It is no wonder we toil all night and take nothing, coming to no solid or dependable conclusions.

Harold Blake Walter

GOODNESS IS ATTRACTIVE

Jesus put reality into religion by a life of goodness that became contagious. Why do we print and circulate more copies of that life that went about doing good than of any other story in all the world? I have liked for years to argue with young people that the most attractive force in the world is goodness. Goodness has to do with our relations with others.

Young people always want to ask, "Then why does evil *seem* so much more attractive than the good?" My answer is that evil seems attractive only when one paints it with colors of the imagination which are not true to fact. I dare anyone to look back upon the evil deeds of yesterday and to believe that they are more attractive than the good that might have been. I came down in a hotel elevator the other day. Two men behind me were talking. One said: "Well, I am not going to drink tonight like I did last night. It leaves such a rotten taste in my mouth and my head feels like a rain barrel." The night before it seemed much more attractive than it did the morning after. A boy came to the University who had no money, so his uncle paid his expenses because of his hope in his nephew. The boy did well for a time until he fell in with some bad company, when he began to "celebrate" at night instead of studying. One night before an examination the group felt it would be more attractive to spend the evening in a tavern than at their study tables. The next morning this young man went to the examination before the effects of the night before had worn off. He was sent home from the class and a few days later was dismissed from the University. When he went home to his local community, disgraced before his family and friends and especially before his uncle, I ask you, was the evil that he followed more attractive than the good that might have been?

J. Walter Malone

THE POWER OF GOODNESS

I believe that goodness is still the most attractive force in the world. A student came to a University in February one year and was pledged to a fraternity after the fall class had been initiated. The young man came downstairs at the fraternity house one Sunday morning a few minutes before eleven and found the living room full of alumni and active members, all dressed in their best. He said "good morning" and started to leave. The president said, "Where are you going?", and he replied that he was going to church. He was then told that he could not go to church that day because they were going to initiate him at eleven o'clock. This young fellow steadied himself and said something like this: "Gentlemen, I always go to church on Sunday morning. I should like very much to be initiated into this group, but I still feel that I must go to church first. I will be back shortly after twelve, and if you are willing to initiate me at that time I shall be glad to have that experience." He went to church and was initiated a little after twelve. That boy was laughed at and razzed with all the good nature of a fraternity group for a couple of years, but in his junior year, when that group was looking for a president, this man was elected to that office. Other things being equal, most groups like for their leaders men who have some quality of goodness and idealism above their own average.

J. Walter Malone

MAN'S SOUL

At the entrance to the beautiful Milan cathedral there are three doors. Over one door are cut roses, with the legend, "That which pleases is but for a moment." Over the door on the other side are cut thorns, with the legend, "That which troubles is but for a moment." But over the central door is cut the cross, with the inscription, "That only is important which endures forever." The light of the moon and of the sun shall be quenched; and the stars at length will go down in dust; but there are two lights death cannot quench—God and the soul. Man is "fearfully and wonderfully made." But the only thing in man upon which God has written the word "Forever" is man's soul.

Clarence Edward Macartney

WHY NATIONS PROSPER

One of the most impressive statements I ever heard was from a South American who was asked why South America had not prospered in spite of its ancient civilization and great natural resources while North America had prospered. He said, "South America was founded by those seeking gold, and North America was founded by those seeking freedom to worship God."

Ensworth Reisner

PRIDE IN HUMILITY

Humility is not one of our outstanding virtues in the United States today. Even if we tried to be humble, we would tend to be proud of it. We're like the member of a certain religious order who was asked what his order stood for, and he answered, "humility." Then he added, "at humility we beat the world." We're more apt to be known in the world for our boasting than for our humility.

Clarence W. Cranford

HUMILITY A GREAT VIRTUE

John Henry Thoreau once said: "Humility, like the darkness reveals heavenly lights." And Daniel Webster wrote:

"Heaven's gates are lower than kings' palaces. One must enter on his knees."

John Robbins Hart

IN THE FATHER'S HOUSE

In our Lord's teaching we learn that "In My Father's house are many mansions: if it were not so, I would have told you. I go to prepare a place for you." Henry Van Dyke once wrote a story called "The Mansions" describing a soul going into the spiritual world and asking to be shown to his mansion. The angel tells him there is no mansion for him, and when he asks why, the angel replies somewhat in these words: "Well, you see, we make the mansions out of the material people send us from the earth, their good deeds, their spiritual power, and you have not sent us any building material."

Send over to that other world your kindness, your goodness, your love, and abide with Him forever.

John Robbins Hart

LIVING WITH YOURSELF

One must live with himself. That may sound easy and most of the time it seems to be a simple process, but for some people and at some periods in life it becomes very difficult. A doctor about to operate on Sam informed him that, "nine out of ten do not live through this operation. Is there anything I can do for you before I begin?" "Yes sir," said Sam, "kindly hand me my hat." No one can hand you your hat. You are caught in the machinery of life. I cannot hand you your hat. You must face the facts of life.

Milton A. Marcy

ALL NIGHT HE CONTINUED IN PRAYER

In the midst of a busy life, pressed upon by crowds, sick in body and in soul who needed His help, important decisions pressing Him such as the one of choosing out the twelve men who would carry his message to the whole world through His church, Jesus, we are told, "went out into the hills to pray; and all night he continued in prayer to God."

His power to heal the sick who came to Him, His wisdom

in choosing the twelve, His creative teaching and His dauntless courage in the face of criticism and persecution, were all dependent upon His prayer life with God. Out in the hills, all night in prayer! But none of these important pressures of His life were the basic reason that He ever and again sought God in prayer. He looked for Him in the lonely hills because He wanted that fellowship. God is best sought for Himself alone. Jesus was fed by prayer, for without God His spirit would have been starved. So I can give you many arguments as to why it would be to your advantage to pray and so develop your spiritual life. But it would be for all the world like telling a young man who is in love with a girl that he should want to marry her because she is a good cook or comes from a good family. What does he care; he marries her because he loves her. He marries her for herself.

So a man prays because he loves God. If I say, prayer will help you to peace and power, to wisdom and to vision, these very practical considerations are really beside the point. For there is but one great reason sufficient in itself. Prayer is the way to know God, to glorify Him, to enjoy Him forever, and this it is we hold to be the chief end of man. For life is not really life at all until it becomes Life in God.

Eugene Carson Blake

THE TEST OF RELIGION

The test of religion is in its practice. "By their fruit ye shall know them." Real religion is harnessed to something, has its feet on the ground. It focuses somewhere. It makes a difference wherever it touches human life. Roland Hill used to say, "I would not give a farthing for a man's religion unless his cat and dog are better for it."

A certain maid when she got religion was asked how she knew she had gotten it. She replied, "Because I no longer sweep the dirt under the rug."

Religion is meant to effect a change in every detail of our lives. There should be no area of life into which God cannot enter.

John Homer Miller

YOU ARE IN DEBT

Whenever you feel particularly low, beset and unjustly mistreated, have you ever sat down and counted the debts you owe to others—debts you cannot possibly pay off? The other evening I was helping my daughter translate some of Caesar's Gallic wars. In my mind's eye I joined Caesar, then a great general, finally the ruler of all Rome. Caesar talked something about the inconvenience of winter weather. It was a chilly evening and my eyes lifted to the thermostat on the wall which kept the room to an even temperature regardless of the weather outside. I pondered the debt that I owed to thousands and millions who had given me the thermostat to which Caesar in all his glory would not have dared to aspire. There were those who had discovered electricity and had come to understand the thermometer and transformed it into a thermostat. There were those who had discovered oil and brought it into usage—the millions of men who had learned how to pipe oil. And, of course, their inventions could not have heated that room had it not been for centuries of work on iron and steel, on rubber-tired trucks, on streets, on cities, on health precautions, on sewage, on piped water, on sanitation. All the inventions and efforts of every man for centuries had concentrated upon that one room and made possible an equitable climate for my comfort. Could I ever repay that debt?

Ah, and what about those who had made possible efforts of those men? A billion women, nursing mothers, scrambling after children, pampering, punishing, feeding, wiping tears and healing hurts. Can any of that be repaid? Would you want to compare your puny efforts with the host of mankind to whom you owe the debt of your very existence? There is not one person who has not incomparably more than the kings of yore. We are debtors all—debtors who cannot possibly pay our just debts to the past.

Ensworth Reisner

CUSTOMS AND PRINCIPLES

There are two elements which emerge in the moral life of mankind; *changing customs,* and *abiding principles.* Some things we do are right because of custom and convention. The laws of etiquette are an example. They change with the times. But some things we do are right because they are right by nature. Some things are final. The laws of arithmetic, for example. Two plus two equals four, not only now, but always. (I have read somewhere that since Einstein established the principle of relativity it is possible that under certain circumstances two plus two may equal five. But as for myself I shall wait for more evidence to come in. In dealing with my bank I shall proceed on the assumption that two plus two equals four, and I furthermore advise everyone to do the same.) Or, the law of gravity. Jump from the tower of a church, and you go down. There is no "maybe" about it. So, too, the Ten Commandments are absolute. They are grounded in the nature of things. They are not true because they are in the Bible. They are in the Bible because they are true. That wonderful insight is conveyed in the Bible story which states that the Decalogue was given to Moses by God. These laws were written by God into the very nature of things. They are vindicated by the experience of the centuries. The laws against killing, against adultery, against theft are basic to the very fabric of social life.

Robert C. Stanger

JUST THREE WORDS

Years ago a distinguished Columbia professor said that Jesus would have just three words to say at a World Disarmament Conference, just three words, "Love your enemy." The nations of the earth do not know peace because the only one who can give them peace they know not. When Christ's goodwill among men is recognized, there will be peace on earth.

John Homer Miller

NO HANDLE ON THE DOOR

There is no possible doubt that the writer of the Book of Revelation saw a vision, for he has given a vision of Jesus Christ that has fascinated the minds of multitudes of Christians. It inspired that beautiful hymn, "O Jesus Thou art standing outside the fast-closed door." It also inspired one of the most appealing pictures of Christ to be found anywhere,

"The Light of the World," by Holman Hunt. The original painting hangs in New College Chapel at Oxford, and it grips the heart of all who gaze upon it seriously.

The figure of Christ fills the canvas. The glowing grace of His presence shines against the darkness; His head is crowned with thorns, but the halo radiates around and above it; one hand is clasping a lantern, but the other is knocking at a door; He is clad in a long, white robe, over which a cloak is thrown. In front of Him a passion vine is growing. The expression on His face is entrancing; it speaks of mingled firmness and sympathy. His eyes captivate our eyes, for whilst those eyes are fixed on us, they seem to peer through the present into the far-distant future. Every little detail of the painting is perfect. The door is hanging on rusty hinges, and covered with the thorny brambles of long years of growth, symbolic of the hearts of men. The artist did not call that picture, "Christ knocking at the door," but, "The Light of the World," and he was right; for the amazing thing is not the knocking at the closed door, but the presence of Him who knocks. He who stands at the door of every heart is nobody less than Christ Himself, the Light of the World.

It is recorded that when Hunt had completed his painting, a friend came into the studio to inspect it. He admired its exquisite grace, and saw at once its spiritual significance, then he turned to the artist, "It is very beautiful, but there is one mistake. You have forgotten to put any handle to the door." The artist explained that that was no mistake, for had there been any handle on the outside, Christ would have turned it and entered. This was a door that could only be opened from the inside. "If any man will open to Me, I will come in and sup with him."

Hunt was right again. Since Calvary the salvation of every man depends not upon Christ, but upon the man himself. The man must open the door of his own heart; he must accept the gift of salvation; he must receive the Christ. If we are waiting for some marvelous experience to come into our lives that shall be irresistible, when Christ will force Himself upon us and burst open that closed door of our heart, I want to tell you that that hour will never come. "If any man will open the door" is the one condition of all divine blessing. The sunshine is a very wonderful creation, but it will never open any shutters for you. YOU must open them—a very simple thing—and all the majesty of light will flood the room. Our shame is that we just will not do that simple thing—open our heart to Christ, and let His everlasting sunshine illumine our whole lives. Holman Hunt himself found Christ through his own painting, for he was not a devout believer at the beginning. When he finished it, he humbly inscribed on the back of the canvas, for no one else to see, "My quoque praetermisso, Domine," "Pass me not by, Lord." Devoted to his calling, led by his mastering subject, true to his art, he sought and found the Christ-life that he portrayed.

Alfred William Price

WHEN TROUBLE COMES

"Regardless of how intellectual we may become, when suffering overtakes us we feel that God has forsaken us, or more specifically that he is actually punishing us."

Now that's not my statement. That's a quotation from the writing of one of our best known specialists in Christian counseling. I don't know how true it is; but if it does express the way many of you feel in time of trouble, it's too bad. Because it simply isn't true that when suffering comes it is a sign that God either has forsaken or is punishing us . . .

Just what is the relation of God to suffering, and to us in our suffering? Let me say it simply and directly: suffering is not a punishment of God; it is a part of our life which God simply has to accept, just as we do. And far from forsaking us in our time of trouble, God is never nearer to us than when we need Him most. And He is never more understanding than when we are suffering . . . after all, He has been through plenty Himself!

An occasion of suffering does not represent the specific will of God, as if He had said, "Well, it's time now for Mary and John to have a little trouble. Suppose I send them this sorrow." What do I mean when I say that suffering is a part of our life which God has to accept just as we do?

There are two aspects of human existence which God maintains, along with whatever consequences may result. One is the dependability of our universe. There are certain regularities in life which seem to be necessary for existence: the movements of earth, sun and moon, the processes of conception and birth, life and death, and all the uniformities of the physical world upon which our very life is based.

These regular activities sometimes cause accidents: storms are brewed, rocks fall; two speeding cars try to occupy the same space—unsuccessfully; something goes wrong in the development of an embryo; a child falls and injures himself. Disease and death seem to be a part of this whole process. And God cannot interfere with this cosmic operation every time one of His children is about to get hurt. If He did this, He would ruin the whole order of the world, which seems to be absolutely necessary to life. To call natural accidents "acts of God" may be proper legal terminology, but it's mighty poor theology.

God simply has to maintain the regularity of the world He has made. And when His children are hurt by it, I suspect that He regrets it, but must restrain Himself from upsetting the whole business.

Another aspect of our life which God has pledged Himself to maintain is our freedom. Much of our suffering is due to our own unwise behaviour. It isn't God's fault if we eat and drink too much and ruin our system. It isn't His fault that we can't get along with each other and in the process of our wars, kill millions of one another's children. I'm sure God doesn't like this any more than we do; but to prevent it would destroy our human freedom, make us mere puppets. And that God will never do . . .

What then is God's relation to us in our trouble? Has He forsaken us? Never. When we need Him most is exactly when He is closest to us. When we are most confused and troubled, is exactly when He is most understanding. When we are most despairing is just when He can be most helpful.

God Himself is no stranger to suffering. This is one of the meanings of the life, passion and death of our Lord. These experiences of Christ are caught up in the life of God Himself . . .

God does not casually observe our suffering from some cold

position far removed from our pain. He has been through all this; He knows how desperately we need His help; and He is right with us to give us what we need.

Best of all—and this is one of the great affirmations of our faith—God is able to help us triumph over pain and suffering. Just as in Christ He overcame death, so He is able to bring joy out of our suffering, happiness out of our pain, good out of evil.

We should never hesitate to trust God in this. He has proven His power; the resurrection of Christ stands as the seal of His victory over pain and death. We can rely on Him.

One of the great words of Jesus was spoken to His disciples at the Last Supper. He knew that many difficulties lay before them; but He knew that they could triumph over them all. So He said, "In the world you shall have tribulation; but be of good cheer. I have overcome the world." So He would say to us: You will have plenty of trouble; but be of good cheer—I have overcome and so can you.

Chester A. Pennington

ABIDE WITH ME

The Reverend Henry Francis Lyte, the rector of the little fishing village of Brixham in Devonshire, will be remembered for all time for his hymn of immortable comfort,—

> Abide with me; fast falls the eventide;
> The darkness deepens; Lord with me abide;
> When other helpers fail and comforts flee,
> Help of the helpless, O abide with me.

This was Lyte's swan-song, written in the Valley of the Shadow. He was stricken with tuberculosis, and had been ordered to the south of France. After Sunday evening service in the little parish church, he was strolling along the shore he loved so well. Then it was that he heard the "Voiceless Whisper of the Great Unseen," and that same night the hymn was completed. He left home the next morning, never to return. In the English Cemetery at Nice his grave is marked by a marble cross.

I fear no foe, with Thee at hand to bless;
Ills have no weight, and tears no bitterness.
Where is death's sting? where grave, thy victory?
I triumph still, if Thou abide with me.

This was the message of a man of God as he stood looking out o'er the ocean of life on the brink of eternity, and facing God unoffended and unafraid, and in it we may find the answer to the purpose of profit and pain. We all shrink from the touch of sorrow, but it shapes us into nobleness and divinity as the chisel, the statue of the sculptor.

Alfred William Price

HOW WE USE TIME

More important than the passing of the years is what we have done with them. Time does nothing but pass away. It is foolish to say, "time will tell," "time will heal," "time will bring out possibilities in him." Time will do nothing of the sort. Time will only come and go. Time does not help a man to help himself. How we use time is what matters.

Vere V. Loper

IS IT NOTHING TO YOU?

As we continue through this Lenten season of sensitive and deep feeling and come to the day of the Crucifixion, to the Cross of Calvary, there is an ancient word which always seems to me to convey the meaning of Good Friday in a specially helpful way. It comes from the old book of *Lamentations.* Many verses might be selected from the New Testament to portray the meaning of the day of the atoning sacrifice, but I think it means even more to be able to reach so far back into history, into the days of the old prophets and from that far off past repeat: "Is it nothing to you, all ye that pass by, come and see if there be any sorrow like unto My sorrow." Think how many there are who always pass by and who never care, or who once cared but are now bereft of that spiritual grace. Say these words each day and you will not pass by but will kneel at the foot of the Cross. "Is it nothing to you, all ye that pass by?"

John Robbins Hart

ROADBLOCKS IN LIFE

There are many roadblocks in life. Haughty Pride is one. Some pride is good, but haughty pride is bad. It so bloats a man with a sense of his own importance that he becomes blind to his own sins until he feels the need of nothing—not even God's forgiveness. Such pride takes many forms—wealth, power, intellect, piety. And piety is the worst because it is so hypocritical.

Another roadblock is Personal Injustice. Here Jesus is crystal clear. "If thou bring thy gift to the altar and there rememberest that thy brother hath ought against thee leave there thy gift before the altar, and go thy way: first be reconciled to thy brother, and then come and offer thy gift."

Another roadblock is Unforgiveness, which is the reverse of Injustice. Injustice is what you have done to another. Unforgiveness is your resentment for what he has done to you. But as a Christian one must hold no resentment against another, though he may still hate the evil deed itself. "If ye forgive not men their trespasses neither will your heavenly Father forgive you your trespasses." There is nothing arbitrary here. It is only the working of a spiritual law.

How can we avoid building spiritual roadblocks against God, or remove them when they are built? By cultivating our Lord's spirit of humility. Humility is the opposite of haughty pride and the only power in man that can overcome it. "Take my yoke upon you," said Jesus, "and learn of me, for I am meek and lowly in heart." Perhaps we are amazed at the lack of humility in our Lord's first disciples. But how about ourselves? At least those first followers did finally learn humility—after Calvary and Pentecost.

A second way to overcome haughty pride is by being honest with ourselves. The great trouble with the Pharisee in the temple was blindness to his own sins. How many people today are likewise self-deceived and need to remember it. James' admonition—"Be ye doers of the word and not hearers only, deceiving your own selves." We must constantly examine ourselves in the light of Christ and ask God to help us be honest with ourselves.

Alvin Lamar Wills

IS THERE ANY WORD FROM GOD?

A glance at history since the 1900's will show a very subtle, and yet a very dramatic change in the thought patterns of people who are connected with the Christian religion. There was a time in the beginning of the Twentieth Century when Science was lifted up and almost deified, a time when the Church began to forsake the authority of the Scriptures and to find not in the Eternal Cross of Christ, but in the crucible of the laboratory, final truth. A time when many pulpits and most Chairs of Philosophy accepted the concept of the inevitability of progress. We were on an escalator that would bring us sure and certain into the Kingdom. The findings of Science, the progress of Society, would be the panacea for all the problems that confronted mankind. We were told to be silent about the sinfulness of human personality. We were to go back to the philosophers of the Renaissance and to the early Greek Sophists and there to learn again that man was the measure of all things.

Swinburne might sing, "Glory to man in the highest," but something began to happen in our world. We found ourselves engaged in so many wars that we no longer named them. We began to number them. We found that Science, capable of devising a scalpel and placing it in the hands of a trained surgeon could cut out a cancer. We found also that Science could design an atom bomb that could unleash the furies of hell, burn to a crisp little children, and cause entire islands to disappear. We found that the escalator of progress sometimes broke down, that depressions came, that people suffered, that man's inhumanity to man was made all the more pointed because of the gifts of the modern world.

People found themselves asking not for views or opinions or syrupy advice, but much more basic questions: Is there any word from God? It is precisely at this point that the Christian Gospel finds its relevance. Jesus Christ shattered history with the explosive word, "Before Abraham was, I was," and He said that there is healing for humanity's hurt. It comes not from man's side, but from God's. It finds its deepest therapy in the statement of the theme, "I am determined not to know anything among you, save Jesus Christ and him crucified." The cross once again towers o'er the wrecks of time and invites all who will to come for salvation and healing.

Robert J. Lamont

YOU CAN TAKE IT WITH YOU

Every promise of the New Testament seems to be that we can lay up treasures and find in them eternal values and hear the words, "Come ye blessed . . . , inherit the kingdom." It is all stored up, you have taken it with you.

Take time, for example. How time slips away through our fingers! Where is yesterday or that hour that slipped past me this morning? Longfellow asked, "What is time? Is it the shadow on a dial, the striking of a clock, the running of the sand through the glass, day and night, summer and winter? No, time is the life of the soul," he says, "and, if not, then what is it?"

We buried the remains of a grand old man of eighty-one the other day. He had lived a life of service, of love and kindness. This past year he worked on a committee for underprivileged children in the community. I am sure that he has taken much of his time with him. Listen to Jesus, "I was sick, and ye visited me; I was in prison, and ye came unto me." Time used, but it was time saved up. Your time spent and given away is all saved up. Jesus insisted that if time is rightly used, you *can* take it with you.

J. Walter Malone

THE IMPORTANCE OF THE HOME

In days gone by when most families had woodsheds and chickencoops, a mother tried to persuade her boy to go up to bed. Finally she said: "See! the little chickens went to sleep a long time ago." Her little son answered: "I know, mother. I have been watching them, and you know what? The mother hen always goes up first."

Children usually follow in the footsteps of their parents. That's why the home is so important, and Jesus appreciated the values of the home. At Bethany He enjoyed staying at the home of Mary and Martha and Lazarus. At Emmaus He gladly accepted the invitation of the two disciples who constrained Him saying: "Abide with us, for it is toward evening and the day is far spent."

Jesus comes to you and to me and pleads: "Behold, I stand at the door and knock: if any man hear my voice and open the door, I will come in to him and will sup with him and he with me."

Paul Splett

TWO IMPOSTORS—TRIUMPH AND DISASTER

Kipling is reputed to have written his poem "If" with his own son primarily in mind. Standing before the boy, he sets forth the conditions of true manhood. One of his conditions is voiced in the familiar words,

> "If you can meet with triumph and disaster
> And treat those two impostors just the same."

In these words, the insight of Kipling is very revealing of an aspect of life which is not always clear to some of us. We are quick to discern the dangers of failure, of disaster. We are not so aware of the menace of triumph and success. Triumph and disaster may require different treatments on the fringe. But, basically, they are both impostors suggesting much that is not true, distorting our understanding and sending us off on vicious and dangerous tangents. They frequently call for the same treatment.

Paul makes a fundamental approach to the problem which Kipling poses. Instead of giving advice to others, he was speaking of what he had been able to do with his own life when he said, "I have learned, in whatever state I am, to be content. I know how to be abased, and I know how to abound; in any and all circumstances I have learned the secret of facing plenty and hunger, abundance and want. I can do all things in Him who strengthens me."

I can recall a comment of a college friend who was looking

at a small box of medals which I had accumulated in athletics. His comment was, "some day you will forget all about those medals unless perhaps your children discover them and cut their teeth on them." I lived to see the literal fulfillment of that prophecy before our first child had acquired much skill in locomotion. So it is with the many victories of life, so important at the moment. That high moment is followed quickly by discouragement and defeat. People see to it that we are deflated—very quickly at times. If they do not, we forget the high moments in the onward rush of events. The triumph which seemed to speak for life proves to be an impostor, heralding only a passing moment. The defeat, the seeming disaster, is soon a tiny speck on a far horizon from which we are moving farther and farther away.

Success is nevertheless but an indication that we have found a path by which we can advise with confidence of attainment. The moment we stop to admire our victory, we make a dead-end street of it—leading nowhere.

Some time ago I saw a picture which interested me very much. It depicted a football player dressed for the game sitting on a bench at the fifty-yard line. He was the only figure in a large stadium upon which winter had come. The picture may have many interpretations. In part, it seemed to indicate the pathos of a man who could not pull himself away from the scenes of his athletic triumph to face the facts of life and move on. He tarried so that he might feast his soul on the memory of the applause of the thousands of yesterday. But meanwhile life had pressed on, and he was left behind. Kipling has another line for such:

"Go to your work and be strong, halting not in your ways,
Balking the end half-won for an instant dole of praise."

The victories of yesterday are but incidents. It remains for us to see that they are incidents in the onward march of life.

Vere V. Loper

REMEMBER ME

What a sublime conclusion to the ministry of our Saviour was His interview with that dying robber on the cross? There was nothing in his life to which this doomed and suffering criminal could appeal as commending him to the mercy of God, for when he rebuked his mocking and cursing brother thief, he said to him: "Dost not thou fear God, seeing thou art in the same condemnation? And we, indeed, justly, for we receive the due reward of our deeds." But when he threw himself upon the mercy of God, and prayed to Jesus, "Remember me when thou comest in thy kingdom," Jesus said to him, "Today shalt thou be with me in Paradise." Thus it came to pass that the first soul to enter heaven after Jesus had made Atonement for sin on the Cross, was that dying thief.

After this great example of sin, repentance, and forgiveness, can anyone doubt that by the great mercy of God, he can conquer his past?

Clarence Edward Macartney

THE PROBLEM

A college professor was lecturing on geography. He explained to the class the great expanse and the vast territory of the State of Texas. One of the students asked him: "Professor, do you think that the whole population of the United States could be put into the State of Texas?" The professor thought for a moment. Then he said: "Yes, if they were all friends." That is the problem. "If they were friends!" That really is the nub of our world's problem today. How can we live together on this crowded earth, so many billions of us, unless we are friends? We live by love. Jesus emphasized that. Recall His statement to His disciples: "No longer do I call you servants, but I have called you friends." He invited people to help to build the "beloved community," the Kingdom of Friends.

Robert C. Stanger

THE POWER OF PRAYER

The great physician, who for nearly 40 years was with the Rockefeller Institute in biological research—Dr. Alexis Carrel, Nobel prize winner and great researcher in cancer, said about prayer, "Prayer is the most powerful form of energy that one can generate." Think of all the energy—now we even have atomic energy, but he says prayer is the *most powerful* form. "The influence of prayer on the human mind is as demonstrable as that of the secreting glands," and then he goes on to say, "results are measured in increased physical buoyancy, greater intellectual vigor, and deeper moral stamina. As a physician, I have seen men after all other therapy has failed, lifted out of disease and melancholy by the serene effort of prayer. "When we pray, we link ourselves with the inexhaustible motive power that spins the universe."

Robert A. Edgar

BEING SOMEBODY

Jesus teaches us that joy and happiness depend on the kind of a person you are. Happiness is in *being* somebody, not in just *having* things. If you will read Jesus' sayings, you will find again and again that he says something like this: Unless what you *are* is greater than anything you *have,* you have lost your life. "What shall it profit a man if he gain the whole world and lose his own soul?"

J. Walter Malone

JUSTICE AND MERCY

Justice alone is not enough. There must also be mercy. Justice seeks to give each man his due, but it also seeks to give us our just deserts when we have broken the law. Mercy, on the other hand, gives us another chance. Justice passes sentence upon us. Mercy grants us a pardon. If God were only just, who, then, could have any hope? For we all deserve punishment and death. Our hope rests on God's mercy who has said, "Though your sins be as scarlet, they shall be as white as snow; though they be red like crimson, they shall be as wool."

No, it is not enough to have justice in the world, we must have forgiveness and love as well. It isn't enough just to say, "with liberty and justice for all." That in itself is a tremendous advance over the treatment accorded to people in most of the world. But we must have genuine love for our fellowmen or we will never strive to see that they get justice.

Clarence W. Cranford

WHEN THE CHURCH IS DEAD

Charles Haddon Spurgeon once looked over his vast congregation and asked, "Have you read 'The Ancient Mariner'? I dare say you thought it one of the strangest imaginations ever put together—dead men pulling the rope; dead men steering. But do you know that I have lived to see that in my lifetime. I have seen a dead man in the pulpit, a dead man as deacon, a dead man handling the plate and a dead man sitting in the pew to hear."

Let us beware lest we become dead spiritually. Such a church excites the contempt of the world.

John S. Wimbish

THE ROLE OF MONEY

Money is the modern miracle-working sacrifice. In days of old, artists and artisans gave themselves and their talents that the great churches might be built. They labored long, without pay, and some few furnished such money as was needed for materials. But quarry men quarried the stone; stone masons laid the stone; artists carved the statues and decorated the churches; painters painted great pictures on the walls and ceilings of the churches; artists in stone and wood made the Altars and other furniture. And they thus gave themselves to the praise and glory of God.

Each of us can do this even today, though we have no such skills; for money is a symbol of life—as money can be earned only by the investment of life in it. Even if people live on the interest from their investments, yet the money that is used to pay the interest must be earned by someone who labors, and thus even this money becomes a symbol of life. When we spend money, we spend life. Money is the sacrificial way in which we do our duty towards God and towards our neighbor.

Don Frank Fenn

SUCCESSFUL FAILURE

Christ said to the eleven apostles who remained faithful: "Ye are they who have continued with Me in My temptations. And I appoint unto you a Kingdom, as My Father hath appointed unto Me." If He could say that to the eleven, He can and will say it to every one who has tried to be true to His teachings.

I emphasize that an honest endeavor is accounted for as worthy in the sight of GOD. He does not expect perfection, but He has every right to expect us to try. No life is complete until a deeper and greater life is put under the human soul—a life into which we can retreat when the world becomes too oppressive.

A fall is never a failure. Only by failures can we measure our growth.

Simon Peter could be called a successful failure. He was impetuous, swore lustily on occasion, thought very well of himself, denied that he knew Christ, when danger came; but (and here is the gist of the whole matter), when he came to himself, he went out and wept bitterly at his failures. He had an undergirding which would not permit his soul to remain sterile. GOD was in him.

William Clyde Howard

EVERYDAY LIFE

Twenty-five years ago Sir Wilfred Grenfell, the great Labrador missionary doctor, wrote a little book entitled, "What Christ Means to me," and on the 6th page he wrote these words, "Christ meant a mother who brought Him right into our family life just by doing daily what He would do in her place." That is what Christ meant to him—a mother who brought Christ down out of theory into every-day life, who revealed His spirit in her own personality, who never faltered in her expression of His love and mercy and tenderness and thoughtfulness.

Edward Hughes Pruden

STRONG ARMS AND PIERCED HANDS

Norman MacLeod, Minister to Queen Victoria, once declared that he could sum up everything that religion meant to him, in a single sentence. "There is a Father in Heaven who loves us, a Brother Saviour who died for us, a Spirit who helps us to be good, and a Home where we shall meet at last."

In this age of rival doctrines, which only bedim the senses

and becloud the mind, it would be well for us thus to be able to summarize our faith. With the future ahead of us, a simple creed within our hearts, there should be no desire to cast covert glances over the shoulder, but only an ardent desire to march on into the glories of the Kingdom. We need not be afraid, for we shall receive assistance every step of the way.

Heine once described how he stood before the statue of the Venus de Milo and gazed upon that matchless perfection of grace and beauty. "But," he exclaimed, "she had no arms, though a goddess, to reach out and help poor beaten souls like me."

But Jesus, the Ambassador of GOD, has arms strong enough to lift the universe, and hands—pierced hands—gentler than a mother's when she soothes her child.

William Clyde Howard

THE KEYS TO SUCCESS

An old southern Negro mammy was once asked to what she attributed her success and this is what she said: "Well, when I walks I walks hard, but when I sits I sits loose, and when I sees worry coming I takes a nap." The secret to success. Someone was telling me the other day that he met a friend of his he hadn't seen for a long time; this friend had just recovered from a serious illness, so he inquired: "How are you sleeping these days?" "Well," the convalescent said, "I sleep pretty good nights and not so bad in the morning, but in the afternoons I just twist and turn." What is the secret of success? I suppose everybody would really like to have the answer to that question.

We should recognize that there is a difference between inward and outward success. Outward success is the kind of success most of us are looking for. We do not realize it, but what a person thinks of us, the success in the minds of men about us, usually appeals to us as the most important kind of success.

Outward success is often measured in terms of education and culture. Where did you go to college? What degrees did you get? How much do you know? And then we set the man up on a pedestal or put him down in the basement, depending upon how much education he has had. Some boys were talking about their dads, how great they were. One boy said: "My Dad is so great he teaches subjects in college which he himself doesn't understand." I imagine you and I took some of those courses way back then.

Too often also we measure success by material possessions. Someone said to me the other day that it takes a successful man to live in this city. You've got to be someone to live here. You've got to make enough money to buy one of these big houses or little houses that have big price tags. Is that a real measure of success? Do all the successful people live here? Do any successful people live down in the slums, the near north side, or out on the plains or prairies, or on the farms? Too often our hats are off to the man who *has* rather than to the person who is. I've heard it said that all the average man wants today is a fairly easy job, a new car, a beautiful wife, and a set of creditors who will listen to reason. That's success—*outward success.*

Now there is a difference between that kind of success and inward success. There's a different standard. Inward or real success is based not on what other people think but what we down deep in our hearts *know,* not on what appears to be on the outside but what deep down in our spirits we really are. What a person does and is, is more important than what he possesses. The rich man was a fool not because he saved up all his grain and built bigger barns, but because he didn't save something else which is far more important. He was successful on the outside; he had all of the grain that he needed for his body and his material well being. Where he made a mistake was when he said: "Soul, thou hast much saved up for thy old age—eat, drink, and be merry." But he hadn't saved anything for his soul, the inner part of man.

At the close of the Civil War a great insurance company got in touch with General Lee and offered him the presidency of the company. Lee thanked them very much for considering him but told them that he knew nothing about insurance. "Well," the spokesman said, "That's perfectly all right; all we want to do is to use your name." Lee picked up his hat and said: "I'm sorry to say my name is not for sale." That's inner success, you see, a quality of life which doesn't deal with outward appearance.

Or there is the city family who wanted to buy a farm. They went into the rural section of Pennsylvania, and found a very fine farm there. This successful business man went to see the farmer and said: "I'm looking for a farm like yours where I could spend my vacations and hunt during the summer." "Well," the farmer replied, "I expect to sell this farm next spring. My wife and I have worked it for forty years; it has become a part of our life, but I don't really believe I could sell it to you." The man said: "Why couldn't you sell it to me?" The farmer replied: "I don't believe you'd understand, but selling this farm to someone who does not aim to farm it, no matter how much you'd give me, would be like selling a herd of young pure bred cattle to a butcher." You see, the farmer was not farming to make money; he was farming to build up a country to feed people.

There's a different standard between outward success and inward success. One doesn't need to labor this point; it is perfectly obvious. The difficulty lies in the fact that all of us want outward success and few of us really realize what inward success can mean, what it will do for us and for other people. We are living in a world where outward success is the measure of success, and inner success is the only real measure for people who understand and are Christians.

Robert A. Edgar

THE GLORY OF THE CROSS

God forbid that I should glory save in the cross of our Lord Jesus Christ, for therein is the assurance of God's forgiving love.

And there is supreme glory in the cross of Jesus because in it we have the manifestation of the life of supreme blessedness. Ay, but there's the rub. Many see the cross, some believe in it, but few glory in it, especially when we realize that it means death to self. It is easy to sing about the sufferings of Christ. It is wonderful to boast of his death for us on the cross. But when we are called upon to enter into the fellowship of his sufferings, to be made conformable to his death, we shrink back. The price is just too great.

Our confessions of faith are so easily spoken and ofttimes so very shallow. I suppose you all know the old story of the young man who was writing a love letter to his sweetheart, boasting of his great love. He wrote, "To show my love for you I would cross the trackless desert, I would brave the burning forest, I would traverse mighty oceans, I would face the Arctic cold," and so on and on. Then, at the end, he added, "P.S. I will be over tomorrow night if it doesn't rain." We laugh at such a story. Yet how many times we speak to Christ in just that way.

"I'll go where you want me to go, dear Lord."
(Of course, that is, if it's a step upward.)
"Over mountain or plain or sea."
(But I would expect to have first-class accommodations.)
"I'll say what you want me to say, dear Lord."
(But please, to an audience that will appreciate my presence.)
"I'll be what you want me to be."
(As long as it doesn't cost too much in personal sacrifice or prestige.)

Sometime ago we had a special meeting in the church and invited an outstanding speaker. He agreed to come, but before the date wrote to say that when he totalled up his expenses he found that he would have only $16.32 left out of the honorarium, which hardly seemed to him adequate recompense for his trip. I believe some adjustment was made, and he came and delivered a magnificent address closing it by saying, "Such is the need of the world without Christ today that I have dedicated my life to do all that is within my power to make the message of the gospel known throughout the world." And I could not help adding to myself, "Yes, if you get more than $16.32 for doing it."

How many times we take the same attitude. We are quite willing to serve Christ so long as we get something out of it and it doesn't cost us too much. The ancient world hated the church and feared the church because it saw in the church a fellowship of self-sacrificing love which if allowed to grow would be the death of worldly society. But today the world does not fear the church, and the church does not give offence to the world, because you can hardly tell the difference between the standard of living of the Christian and the non-Christian. Isn't it strange that we who are followers of Jesus Christ insist on living like kings, when he who is the King of kings lived like a pauper?

It is very easy to rationalize our selfishness. We have to keep up outward appearances, a man should live so that he will command certain respect, everyone has the right to some pleasures. It is easy to rationalize our selfishness, but it is time we eradicated selfishness and faced spiritual realities. How can we pray sincerely for the lost throughout the world when the money we spend for unnecessary trifles could send an army of missionaries out into all the world? How can we honestly ask young people to dedicate their lives in sacrificial service to Christ while we continue to live in luxury and ease that they will never know if they leave all to follow Christ? How can we brazenly profess our love to Christ when we will not accept the shame and the reproach of his cross? John Wesley said, "Give me one hundred preachers who fear nothing but sin and desire nothing but God, and I care not a straw whether they be clergymen or laymen; such alone will shake the gates of hell and set up the Kingdom of heaven on earth." There is glory in so marching in triumph under the banner of the cross though we may be derided as the filth and offscouring of the world. But are there a hundred preachers in this city who are willing thus to suffer the loss of all things that they may know Christ and make him known? Are there a hundred members of this church who are willing thus to embrace the cross, to die to self that Christ might be manifest in you?

O Cross, that liftest up my head,
I dare not ask to fly from thee;
I lay in dust life's glory dead,
And from the ground there blossoms red
Life—do you believe it?
Life—will you receive it?
Life that shall endless be.

When this world shall be dissolved into cosmic dust, and the sun has become a burned-out cinder, when the bands of the constellations have been loosed and the heavens rolled up as a scroll, there will still remain unchanged the cross of Christ, for it is rooted in the heart of God. There will remain the eternal cross and your immortal soul judged, approved or condemned by the Cross. It will be too late then to decide what response you should make. Now is the accepted time, today is the day of salvation. God grant that all of us may accept the cross as the proof of God's power to save, as the assurance of his forgiving love and as the pledge of our self-denying commitment to Christ, that we may say with the apostle, "God forbid that I should glory save in the cross of our Lord Jesus Christ, by whom the world is crucified unto me, and I unto the world."

J. Clyde Henry

A MIND FIXED ON GOD

Mr. Gladstone kept over his desk, when he was the Prime Minister of England, these words that are enfolded in the depths of the Book of Isaiah: "Thou wilt keep in perfect peace him whose mind is stayed on Thee."

John Robbins Hart

PREACHING

A contemporary preacher, writing on the work of the ministry, has well said:

"We are sent not to preach sociology, but salvation;
not economics, but evangelism;
not reform, but redemption;
not culture, but conversion;
not progress, but pardon;
not the new social order, but the new birth;
not revolution, but regeneration;
not renovation, but revival;
not resuscitation, but resurrection;
not a new organization, but a new creation;

not democracy, but the gospel;
not civilization, but Christ.
We are ambassadors, not diplomats."

I am no radio commentator. This pulpit will not be used as a sounding board for all the political intrigue of the world.

Preaching is not an analysis of the news.

I am no Bible lecturer. Preaching is not lecturing. In all real preaching, there is passion and enthusiasm. In order to move you, I myself must be moved.

Richard Baxter used to say, "There is nothing more indecent than a dead preacher, speaking to dead sinners, the living truth of a living God."

John S. Wimbish

ANXIETY IS WITHIN YOU

The Greek word translated, "anxious" has a very interesting derivation. It comes from the root meaning, "to be drawn in two directions." What a marvelous definition of anxiety, "to be pulled apart, trying to do two things at the same time." Jesus says, "Be not therefore anxious about tomorrow, for tomorrow will bring with it its own worries and anxieties. Enough for today is its own troubles." Anxious people are drawn in two directions: their concern about today and their worry about tomorrow at the same time. Jesus' counsel is not to abandon all concern. It is to unify our concern, and focus it upon the point where it will do some good, namely today, for our worries and concerns about tomorrow can be of little value.

Anxiety is something within us and not outside. This is apparently very obvious, but many people try to place the source of their anxiety outside themselves, when it is really a matter of inner attitude and tension, rather than external condition.

The reason so many people fail in their attempts to overcome their anxiety is because they try to fix up conditions outside themselves when the trouble, the real trouble, lies within them. We go through stages in which we try to imagine that we can solve our problems by changing outside conditions. We are like the man who joined the "Don't Worry Club." All they did was to say to themselves, "There's no use worrying! Nobody needs to worry! Don't ever worry! If you worry, you're in trouble." So he wrote this poem, "I've joined the new "Don't Worry Club," and now I hold my breath, I'm so scared for fear I'll worry, that I'm worried most to death." One doesn't meet these inner tensions by trumping up some imaginary way of changing things outside.

The matter of meeting anxiety is a *way of life.* You don't buy it. You don't get it by reading a book. It grows with life! You can meet your anxieties if you will accept and follow this way of life: First of all recognize that the anxiety which is yours is *in* you, not outside. Second, you can master your anxieties only by accepting this way of life which is absolute trust in a creative intelligence which undergirds our universe. Marion Anderson once said to the little girl who offered to do anything to be able to sing like she could sing, "Would you practise eight hours a day?" You, who want to become less anxious and overcome your anxieties, would you be willing to practise the presence of God daily and Sundays? It's a way of life, there are no trick formulas, no special rules. It is a way of life dedicated in trust to this creative intelligence which undergirds our universe.

Robert A. Edgar

BOTH GOOD AND EVIL DEMAND SACRIFICE

Consider this matter of the cost of living, not how much the groceries cost, how much clothes cost, how much everything costs, important as they may be, but the cost of right and the cost of wrong. We do one or the other and both of them have a price. First of all we need to understand that both good and evil, right and wrong, demand some kind of sacrifice. People have the mistaken idea that self-sacrifice is the lot only of those who do good. I suppose when Jesus said: "If any man shall come after me let him deny himself and pick up his cross and follow me," people got the idea that only the good demands sacrifice. However, everything we choose, good or bad, has a price. "Take what you want," says God, "take it and pay for it." The tramp on Skid Row certainly didn't choose good; he chose dissipation, self-indulgence, and what a price he paid! He gave up all the good things in life. George Washington chose to be a leader in our country, to help in its revolutionary program; he paid a price. Benedict Arnold chose another way; but he too paid a price. Jesus Christ chose the way of the cross to bring to our world a new way and path of life. Whether we like it or not, we live in a world which demands a price. For every decision we make we have to be sacrificial, all of us, whether we choose good or evil. There is a universal moral law which says that you cannot make a choice without accepting the consequences; and one cannot outwit the universal law any more than he can outwit the physical law of gravitation.

"Take what you want," says God, "take it, but in the long run you pay for it." Take a look at the world. In one generation we have fought two great world wars. We chose to fight rather than to work out our world relations peacefully. Today we're paying for it. There's a moral law in this universe just as sure and as strong and as real as any of the scientific physical laws by which we live. It follows then, that the first thing in this matter of the cost of right or wrong is that both cost something. The person who does the right is not the only person who is making a sacrifice for often the man who does the wrong makes a far greater sacrifice.

Robert A. Edgar

LOOKING OUT FOR YOURSELF

When some people say, "Well, I must look out for myself; if I don't look out for myself, nobody will," I wonder what self they are thinking of. A number of years ago an American minister explained this in the following illustration: As children we used to have a box of blocks, and when we turned it over, a smaller block would come out. Then, if we turned it back again, a still smaller one would come out until there was a whole row of blocks, a big one at one end and a tiny little one at the other end.

Now, when one says, "I must look out for myself," which

self does he really mean, the little one at the one end or the great big one at the other end? Washington might have saved his Virginia planter self and lost his larger self, the Father of his Country. Jesus might have saved his carpenter of Nazareth self and lost his larger self, the Saviour of the World.

J. Walter Malone

STEALING FROM GOD

"Will a man rob God?" asked the prophet Malachi when he was telling the people to honor God with their neglected tithes. The same question might well be asked concerning God's Day. "Will a man rob God?" A native Chinese preacher, speaking on the subject of robbing God, told of a man who went to market with a string of seven coins. Seeing a beggar who asked for alms, he gave the man six coins, and kept only one for himself. The beggar, instead of being thankful, followed the good man and stole from him the seventh coin also. Miserable ingrate, you say. But how different is that from stealing from God, who has given us the six days for ourselves, the Seventh Day also?

Clarence Edward Macartney

KNOWING THE SHEPHERD

A famous English actor was being honored with a great banquet at the time of his retirement from public life. After dinner, instead of the usual speeches, he offered to recite any dramatic role he had taken that might be requested. There was the usual awkward pause and an old minister near-by, perhaps to start something, asked him if he could recite the Twenty-third Psalm. He thought a moment and then agreed to do so on one condition. That was, that the minister should recite it after him. With some regrets the minister agreed. The actor recited the Twenty-third Psalm with all of his power of oratory, and when he had finished there was a great burst of applause. The minister then began slowly, "The Lord is my shepherd, I shall not want." When he had finished there was no applause, but the story says that some eyes were moist and some heads were bowed. The actor, quickly sensing the situation, put his hand on the minister's shoulder, and said, "I appealed to your ears, but this man appealed to your hearts. I know the Twenty-third Psalm, but this man knows the Shepherd."

J. Walter Malone

CHAPTER IV

EPIGRAMS AND WITTICISMS

The worst tempered people I've ever met were people who knew they were wrong. *Wilson Mizner*

I have never been hurt by anything I didn't say. *Calvin Coolidge*

To be positive:—To be mistaken at the top of one's voice. *Ambrose Bierce*

Expert:—One who knows more and more about less and less. *Nicholas Murray Butler*

Conscience:—An inner voice that warns us somebody is looking. *H. L. Mencken*

The best thing for an argument is not words and ideas, but to stop arguing. *Henry S. Haskins*

Duty is what one expects from others. *Oscar Wilde*

You've no idea what a poor opinion I have of myself—and how little I deserve it. *William S. Gilbert*

What can one possibly introduce into a mind that is full, and full of itself. *Joseph Joubert*

Some people use language to express thought, some to conceal thought, and some instead of thought.

You can't keep trouble from coming, but you needn't give it a chair to sit on. *Old Proverb*

A cure for covetousness: Think of something to give instead of something to get.

No person was ever honored for what he received. Honor has been the reward for what he gave. *Calvin Coolidge*

I am an old man and have known a great many troubles, but most of them never happened. *Mark Twain*

Wouldn't it be nice if we could find other things as easily as we find fault? Then we would all be rich.

One of the heaviest loads to carry is a bundle of bad habits.

When you are in the right, you can afford to keep your temper; when in the wrong, you cannot afford to lose it.

A man could retire nicely in his old age if he could dispose of his experience for what it cost him.

Everyone can give pleasure in some way. One person can do it by coming into a room, and another by going out.

Gossip is like mud thrown against a clean wall; it may not stick, but it leaves a mark.

A great philosopher once said: "A work well done never needs doing over." Wonder if he ever tried weeding his garden.

A man should work eight hours a day and sleep eight hours, but not at the same time.

Pretending to be rich keeps a lot of people poor.

We like people to come right out and say what they think—unless they disagree with us.

These days there are too many people in too many cars in too much of a hurry going in too many directions to nowhere for nothing.

If you don't enjoy what you have now, how can you be happier with more?

An old Chinese philosopher was asked what was the greatest joy he had found in life. "A child," he said, "going down the road singing, after asking me the way."

A penny will hide the whole world, if you hold it close enough to your eye.

The brain is a wonderful thing. It never stops functioning from the time you're born until the moment you stand up to make a speech.

Many a man would tell his troubles to someone else if he did not have to wait for the other fellow to get through telling his first.

The great thing in this world is not so much where we are, but in what direction we are going.

Oliver Wendell Holmes

The fellow who can face the music usually gets to lead the band.

Worry is just like a rocking-horse; it keeps you going, but it gets you nowhere.

If life were as easy as we want it to be, most of us would sleep all the way through it.

A depression is a period when people have to do without what their forefathers never had.

How's this for a motto for all employees to follow: "Make sure you are underpaid."

A mother is a person who, seeing there are only four pieces of pie for five people, promptly announces she never did care for pie.

The best way to keep up with the Joneses is to take it easy for a while—and in a few years you'll meet them coming back.

The man who claims he never made a mistake in his life usually has a wife who did.

A noted orator asked Thomas Jefferson for the richest passage in all literature. He said it was the first sixteen verses of the fifth chapter of Matthew.

Charles Dickens was asked as to the most pathetic story in literature. He said it was that of the prodigal son.

When Daniel Webster was questioned as to what he considered the greatest legal digest, his reply was the Sermon on the Mount.

No one has equaled David for poetry, nor Isaiah for vision, nor Jesus for his moral and ethical teachings, nor Peter for holy zeal, nor Paul for logic, nor John's statement of sanctified love.

The Divine Word of God is the greatest of all books, and its Author the greatest of all teachers. We do well to stay close to its pages. *Sunshine Magazine*

You can't build up a reputation on what you are going to do.

There is no wholly satisfactory substitute for brains, but silence does pretty well.

A small boy is a pain in the neck when he is around, and a pain in the heart when he is not.

Some persons think they have a sense of humor when they laugh at something which would make them mad if it happened to them. *Herbert V. Prochnow*

A person may pay everything he owes in this world and still have a heavy debt to settle in the other world.

Dignity is the cloak we wear to conceal our ignorance.

Civilization is always tottering, but fortunately it keeps tottering forward.

The girl who shines best at the bridge table doesn't always brighten up the house. *Herbert V. Prochnow*

Hardship makes a person either bitter or better.

Most of us will do anything to improve ourselves except what's really necessary.

Sometimes you can help the other fellow by just leaving him alone. *Herbert V. Prochnow*

When discouraged, remember even something that ends unhappily—happily ends.

A man is known by the company he keeps and avoids.

The temperamental person is generally more temper than mental.

When you apologize you always have the last word.
Herbert V. Prochnow

Parents with intelligent children believe in heredity.

Few of us realize how little we deserve the good opinion we have of ourselves.

Ignorance makes prejudices enjoyable.

A poor man can be happy, but no happy man is poor.
Herbert V. Prochnow

You always lose when you quit trying in trying times.

When you tell your troubles to someone else, ask yourself how you would like to listen to his.

It is a mistaken idea that greatness and great success mean the same thing.

There is no shock so great as when a person finds the world can get along without him. *Herbert V. Prochnow*

Hard work makes leisure possible, but you don't have time to use it.

Egotism is what makes some people able to live with themselves.

A man is well-balanced if he can get a lot of money without letting a lot of money get him.

Children have been well trained if they don't have to be coached on how to act when they go to a party.

To train children at home it's necessary for both the parents and children to spend some time there.
Herbert V. Prochnow

No one is ever too old to learn, and that may be why all of us keep putting it off.

The trouble with these "How to Succeed" books is that you find out from them that you have to work for it.
Herbert V. Prochnow

A good many drivers seem to think the speed limit on a highway is what their cars can do.

A loafer is a person who spends his time keeping busy people idle. *Herbert V. Prochnow*

The person who hasn't a leg to stand on is usually the one who does the most kicking.

There are two sides to every question—the wrong side and our side.

Children are natural mimics—they act like their parents in spite of every attempt to teach them good manners.

By the time the youngest children have learned to keep the house tidy, the oldest grandchildren are on hand to tear it to pieces again. *Christopher Morley*

The worst reconciliation is preferable to the best divorce. *Cervantes*

The great secret of successful marriage is to treat all disasters as incidents and none of the incidents as disasters. *Harold Nicolson*

Failure is the path of least persistence.

Tact: the ability to describe others as they see themselves. *Abraham Lincoln*

Tolerance: another word for indifference. *W. Somerset Maugham*

Television: radio with eyestrain.

Grandmother: an old lady who keeps your mother from spanking you.

Conceit: God's gift to little men. *Bruce Barton*

Insomnia: a contagious disease often transmitted from babies to parents. *Shannon Fife*

It's all right to hold a conversation, but you should let go of it now and then. *Richard Armour*

Experience is a name everyone gives to their mistakes.
Oscar Wilde

Flowers have an expression of countenance as much as men or animals. Some seem to smile; some have a sad expression; some are pensive and diffident; others again are plain, honest and upright, like the broadfaced sunflower and the hollyhock.
Henry Ward Beecher

A boy is growing up when he walks around a puddle instead of through it.

Middle age is when you start eating what is good for you instead of what you like.

Happiness is like jam—you can't spread even a little without getting some on yourself.

It is not the possession of good things which brings happiness —it is the ability to enjoy what comes. Happiness is an aptitude.
Bernard Grasset

He has spent all his life in letting down empty buckets into empty wells; and he is frittering away his old age in trying to draw them up again.
Sydney Smith

The only thing worse than having too much to do is not having enough.

I like work; it fascinates me; I can sit and look at it for hours.
Jerome K. Jerome

It has been left to our generation to discover that you can move heaven and earth to save five minutes and then not have the faintest idea what to do with them when you have saved them.
Dr. C. E. M. Joad

To have what you want is riches; but to be able to do without is power.
George Macdonald

The more a man possesses over and above what he uses, the more careworn he becomes.
Bernard Shaw

An optimist sees an opportunity in every calamity; a pessimist sees a calamity in every opportunity.

Everything is funny that happens to somebody else.
Collie Knox

Everyone has something to be modest about.

Everybody thinks of changing humanity and nobody thinks of changing himself. *Tolstoi*

If you want work well done, select a busy man—the other kind has no time. *Elbert Hubbard*

We are always hard on our own faults in others; we know how inexcusable they are. *I. Compton-Burnett*

The happiest man is the man who knows least about himself. *Ethel Mannin*

A man travels the world over in search of what he needs and returns home to find it. *George Moore*

Think of your own faults the first part of the night when you are awake, and of the faults of others the latter part of the night when you are asleep. *Chinese Proverb*

Don't stay away from church because there are so many hypocrites. There's always room for one more. *A. R. Adams*

Conceit may puff a man up, but never prop him up.
John Ruskin

To love oneself is the beginning of a lifelong romance.
Oscar Wilde

Glory lies in the estimation of lookers-on. When lookers-on perish as countless generations have done, glory perishes, as countless glories have done. *Henry S. Haskins*

We judge ourselves by what we feel capable of doing; others judge us by what we have done. *Henry W. Longfellow*

Consider how many do not even know your name, and how many will soon forget it, and how those who now praise you will presently blame you. Fame after death is of no value and neither is reputation now, nor anything else.
Marcus Aurelius

We are so presumptuous that we wish to be known by all the world, and even by people who will live after we are gone, and we are so vain that the good opinion of five or six persons near us delights and contents us. *Blaise Pascal*

It is well, when one is judging a friend, to remember that he is judging you with the same godlike and superior impartiality. *Arnold Bennett*

If you confer a benefit, never remember it; if you receive one, never forget it. *Chilon*

We see more clearly what others fail to do for us than what they actually do.

It is not easy to find happiness in ourselves, and it is not possible to find it elsewhere. *Agnes Repplier*

Men do not stumble over mountains, but over molehills. *Confucius*

If you don't get everything you want, think of the things you don't get that you don't want. *Oscar Wilde*

Every man who is high up loves to think that he has done it all himself; and the wife smiles, and lets it go at that. *J. M. Barrie*

Heredity is an omnibus in which all our ancestors ride, and every now and then one of them puts his head out and embarrasses us. *Oliver Wendell Holmes*

Few men really want justice; what all mankind prays for is mercy.

The measure of a man's real character, is what he would do if he knew he would never be found out. *Thomas B. Macaulay*

Three hints on speech making: Be sincere, be brief, be seated.

Usually the first screw that gets loose in one's head is the one that controls the tongue.

Never get angry because someone knows more than you do; just remember, it isn't his fault.

Plan your future carefully. That's where you're going to spend the rest of your life.

Have patience; all things are difficult before they become easy.

Someone has figured out that home is the place where part of the family waits until the rest of the family brings back the car.

The right temperature at home is more surely maintained by the warm hearts and cool heads of those who live there, than by electric thermostats.

Be careful how you live. You may be the only Bible some people ever read. *From Partners*

Let the other fellow talk once in a while. You can't learn anything listening to yourself.

Education will broaden a narrow mind, but there is no known cure for a big head. *J. Graham*

Mark Twain once said, "When I was fourteen years old, my father was so ignorant I hated to have the old man around. But when I was twenty-one years old, I was astonished to see how much my father had learned in only seven years."

Maybe the reason some youngsters run away from home is that they don't like to stay there alone.

Some persons are like roosters who believe the sun rises each day to hear them crow.

No matter how little a little man gets he never feels little. No matter how great a great man gets he never feels great.

The joy of motherhood is what mother experiences when all the youngsters are in bed.

Mothers who scold little boys for carrying crazy things in their pockets should look in their handbags.

If you would like to leave footprints in the sands of time, you had better wear work shoes.

Children between 4 and 17 are at their mental peaks. At 4 they know all the questions; at 17 they know all the answers.

CHAPTER V

QUOTATIONS FROM LITERATURE

ADVERSITY

Adversity is the diamond dust Heaven polishes its jewels with. *Leighton*

I never met with a single instance of adversity which I have not in the end seen was for my good. I have never heard of a Christian on his deathbed complaining of his afflictions.
A. Proudfit

He that has no cross will have no crown. *Quarles*

No life is so hard that you can't make it easier by the way you take it. *Ellen Glasgow*

ADVICE

He that gives good advice, builds with one hand; he that gives good counsel and example, builds with both; but he that gives good admonition and bad example, builds with one hand and pulls down with the other. *Bacon*

It is easy when we are in prosperity to give advice to the afflicted. *Aeschylus*

AFFLICTION

If your cup seems too bitter, if your burden seems too heavy, be sure that it is the wounded hand that is holding the cup, and that it is He who carries the cross that is carrying the burden. *S. I. Prime*

No Christian but has his Gethsemane; but every praying Christian will find there is no Gethsemane without its angel.
T. Binney

AGE

When we are young, we are slavishly employed in procuring something whereby we may live comfortably when we grow old; and when we are old, we perceive it is too late to live as we proposed. *Pope*

Old age is a blessed time. It gives us leisure to put off our earthly garments one by one, and dress ourselves for heaven. "Blessed are they that are home-sick, for they shall get home."
R. Palmer

A comfortable old age is the reward of a well-spent youth.—Instead of its bringing sad and melancholy prospects of decay, it should give us hopes of eternal youth in a better world.
R. Palmer

AMBITION

Fling away ambition. By that sin angels fell. How then can man, the image of his Maker, hope to win by it?
Shakespeare

Ambition is so powerful a passion in the human breast, that however high we reach we are never satisfied. *Machiavelli*

Too low they build who build below the skies. *Young*

ANGER

The fire you kindle for your enemy often burns yourself more than him. *Chinese Proverb*

Life appears to me too short to be spent in nursing animosity or registering wrong. *Charlotte Brontë*

Consider how much more you often suffer from your anger and grief, than from those very things for which you are angry and grieved. *Marcus Antoninus*

ANXIETY

Anxiety is the rust of life, destroying its brightness and weakening its power.—A childlike and abiding trust in Providence is its best preventive and remedy. *Tryon Edwards*

Anxiety is a word of unbelief or unreasoning dread.—We have no right to allow it. Full faith in God puts it to rest.
Horace Bushnell

ASPIRATION

God has never ceased to be the one true aim of all right human aspirations. *Vinet*

There are glimpses of heaven to us in every act, or thought, or word, that raises us above ourselves. *A. P. Stanley*

AUTUMN

The leaves in autumn do not change color from the blighting touch of frost, but from the process of natural decay. They fall when the fruit is ripened, and their work is done. And their splendid coloring is but their graceful and beautiful surrender of life when they have finished their summer offering of service to God and man. And one of the great lessons the fall of the leaf teaches, is this: Do your work well, and then be ready to depart when God shall call. *Tryon Edwards*

BENEFICENCE

God has so constituted our nature that we cannot be happy unless we are, or think we are, the means of good to others. We can scarcely conceive of greater wretchedness than must be felt by him who knows he is wholly useless in the world.

Erskine Mason

I never knew a child of God being bankrupted by his benevolence. What we keep we may lose, but what we give to Christ we are sure to keep. *T. L. Cuyler*

BENEVOLENCE

In this world it is not what we take up, but what we give up, that makes us rich. *H. W. Beecher*

The disposition to give a cup of cold water to a disciple, is a far nobler property than the finest intellect. *Howells*

Just in proportion as a man becomes good, divine, Christ-like, he passes out of the region of theorizing into the region of benevolent activities. It is good to think well; it is divine to act well. *H. Mann*

BIBLE

The longer you read the Bible, the more you will like it; it will grow sweeter and sweeter; and the more you get into the spirit of it, the more you will get into the spirit of Christ.

Romaine

Scholars may quote Plato in their studies, but the hearts of millions will quote the Bible at their daily toil, and draw strength from its inspiration, as the meadows draw it from the brook. *Conway*

The Bible is one of the greatest blessings bestowed by God on the children of men. It has God for its author; salvation for its end, and truth without any mixture for its matter. It is all pure, all sincere; nothing too much; nothing wanting.

Locke

When you have read the Bible, you will know it is the word of God, because you will have found it the key to your own heart, your own happiness and your own duty.

Woodrow Wilson

I believe a knowledge of the Bible without a college course is more valuable than a college course without a Bible.

William Lyon Phelps

All that I am I owe to Jesus Christ, revealed to me in His divine Book. *David Livingstone*

Do you know a book that you are willing to put under your head for a pillow when you lie dying? That is the book you want to study while you are living. There is but one such book in the world. *Joseph Cook*

There is a Book worth all other books which were ever printed. *Patrick Henry*

I speak as a man of the world to men of the world; and I say to you, Search the Scriptures! The Bible is the book of all others, to be read at all ages, and in all conditions of human life; not to be read once or twice or thrice through, and then laid aside, but to be read in small portions of one or two chapters every day, and never to be intermitted, unless by some overruling necessity. *J. Q. Adams*

Give to the people who toil and suffer, for whom this world is hard and bad, the belief that there is a better made for them. Scatter Gospels among the villages, a Bible for every cottage. *Victor Hugo*

A Bible and a newspaper in every house, a good school in every district—all studied and appreciated as they merit—are the principal support of virtue, morality, and civil liberty. *Franklin*

BOOKS

Except a living man there is nothing more wonderful than a book! a message to us from the dead—from human souls we never saw, who lived, perhaps, thousands of miles away. And yet these, in those little sheets of paper, speak to us, arouse us, terrify us, teach us, comfort us, open their hearts to us as brothers. *Charles Kingsley*

Books are the legacies that genius leaves to mankind, to be delivered down from generation to generation, as presents to those that are yet unborn. *Addison*

Choose an author as you choose a friend. *Roscommon*

The book to read is not the one which thinks for you, but the one which makes you think. No book in the world equals the Bible for that. *McCosh*

BROTHERHOOD

Whoever in prayer can say, "Our Father," acknowledges and should feel the brotherhood of the whole race of mankind. *Tryon Edwards*

There is no brotherhood of man without the fatherhood of God. *H. M. Field*

If God is thy father, man is thy brother. *Lamartine*

CHARACTER

Let us not say, Every man is the architect of his own fortune; but let us say, Every man is the architect of his own character.
G. D. Boardman

Talents are best nurtured in solitude; character is best formed in the stormy billows of the world. *Goethe*

A man's character is the reality of himself. His reputation is the opinion others have formed of him. Character is in him; reputation is from other people—that is the substance, this is the shadow. *H. W. Beecher*

A man may be outwardly successful all his life long, and die hollow and worthless as a puff-ball; and he may be externally defeated all his life long, and die in the royalty of a kingdom established within him. A man's true estate of power and riches, is to be in himself; not in his dwelling, or position, or external relations, but in his own essential character. That is the realm in which he is to live, if he is to live as a Christian man. *H. W. Beecher*

CHARITY

A man should fear when he enjoys only the good he does publicly. Is it not publicity rather than charity, which he loves? Is it not vanity, rather than benevolence, that gives such charities? *H. W. Beecher*

To pity distress is but human; to relieve it is Godlike.
H. Mann

My poor are my best patients. God pays for them.
Boerhaave

CHEERFULNESS

You have not fulfilled every duty unless you have fulfilled that of being cheerful and pleasant. *C. Buxton*

If I can put one touch of a rosy sunset into the life of any man or woman, I shall feel that I have worked with God.
G. Macdonald

Burdens become light when cheerfully borne. *Ovid*

CHILDREN

The child is father of the man. *Wordsworth*

I love these little people; and it is not a slight thing, when they, who are so fresh from God, love us. *Dickens*

Children have more need of models than of critics. *Joubert*

What gift has Providence bestowed on man that is so dear to him as his children? *Cicero*

Children are God's apostles, sent forth, day by day, to preach of love, and hope and peace. *J. R. Lowell*

A torn jacket is soon mended, but hard words bruise the heart of a child. *Longfellow*

When a child can be brought to tears, not from fear of punishment, but from repentance for his offence, he needs no chastisement. When the tears begin to flow from grief at one's own conduct, be sure there is an angel nestling in the bosom. *A. Mann*

What the best and wisest parent wants for his own child that must the community want for all its children. *John Dewey*

Children do not know how their parents love them, and they never will till the grave closes over those parents, or till they have children of their own. *Cooke*

CHRISTIAN

Christ is the great central fact in the world's history; to him everything looks forward or backward. All the lines of history converge upon him. All the march of providence is guided by him. All the great purposes of God culminate in him. The greatest and most momentous fact which the history of the world records is the fact of his birth. *Spurgeon*

One truly Christian life will do more to prove the divine origin of Christianity than many lectures. It is of much greater importance to develop Christian character than to exhibit Christian evidences. *J. M. Gibson*

It does not require great learning to be a Christian and be convinced of the truth of the Bible. It requires only an honest heart and a willingness to obey God. *Barnes*

The Christian needs a reminder every hour; some defeat, surprise, adversity, peril; to be agitated, mortified, beaten out of his course, so that all remains of self will be sifted out.
Horace Bushnell

The best advertisement of a workshop is first-class work. The strongest attraction to Christianity is a well-made Christian character. *T. L. Cuyler*

CHRISTIANITY

Christianity is not a theory or speculation, but a life; not a philosophy of life, but a life and a living process. *Coleridge*

The task and triumph of Christianity is to make men and nations true and just and upright in all their dealings, and to bring all law, as well as all conduct, into subjection and conformity to the law of God. *H. J. Van Dyke*

There's not much practical Christianity in the man who lives on better terms with angels and seraphs, than with his children, servants, and neighbors. *H. W. Beecher*

Christianity is . . . not a philosophy of life, but a life and a living process. *S. T. Coleridge*

CONSCIENCE

He will easily be content and at peace whose conscience is pure. *Thomas a Kempis*

Conscience is merely our own judgment of the right or wrong of our actions, and so can never be a safe guide unless enlightened by the word of God. *Tryon Edwards*

Conscience tells us that we ought to do right, but it does not tell us what right is—that we are taught by God's word.
H. C. Trumbull

CONTENTMENT

Resign every forbidden joy; restrain every wish that is not referred to God's will; banish all eager desires, all anxiety; desire only the will of God; seek him alone and supremely, and you will find peace. *Fenelon*

I am always content with what happens; for I know that what God chooses is better than what I choose. *Epictetus*

My God, give me neither poverty nor riches, but whatsoever it may be Thy will to give, give me, with it, a heart that knows humbly to acquiesce in what is Thy will. *Gotthold*

DEATH

We picture death as coming to destroy; let us rather picture Christ as coming to save. We think of death as ending; let us rather think of life as beginning, and that more abundantly. We think of losing; let us think of gaining. We think of parting, let us think of meeting. We think of going away; let us think of arriving. And as the voice of death whispers "You must go from earth," let us hear the voice of Christ saying, "You are but coming to Me!" *N. Macleod*

No man who is fit to live need fear to die. To us here, death is the most terrible thing we know. But when we have tasted its reality it will mean to us birth, deliverance, a new creation of ourselves. It will be what health is to the sick man; what home is to the exile; what the loved one given back is to the bereaved. As we draw near to it a solemn gladness should fill our hearts. It is God's great morning lighting up the sky. Our fears are the terror of children in the night. The night with its terrors, its darkness, its feverish dreams, its passing away; and when we awake it will be into the sunlight of God. *Fuller*

Men may live fools, but fools they cannot die. *Young*

Let death be daily before your eyes, and you will never entertain any abject thought, nor too eagerly covet anything. *Epictetus*

Death and love are the two wings that bear the good man to heaven. *Michelangelo*

How shocking must thy summons be, O death, to him that is at ease in his possessions! who, counting on long years of pleasure here, is quite unfurnished for the world to come. *Blair*

Our friend and we were invited abroad on a party of pleasure, which is to last forever. His chair was ready first, and he is gone before us. We could not all conveniently start together; and why should you and I be grieved at this, since we are soon to follow, and know where to find him. *Benjamin Franklin*

Good-night! good-night! as we so oft have said,
  Beneath this roof at midnight, in the days
  That are no more, and shall no more return.
Thou hast but taken up thy lamp and gone to bed;
  I stay a little longer, as one stays
  To cover up the embers that still burn.
Henry Wadsworth Longfellow

DESPAIR

He that despairs measures Providence by his own little contracted model and limits infinite power to finite apprehensions. *South*

It is impossible for that man to despair who remembers that his Helper is omnipotent. *Jeremy Taylor*

DISAPPOINTMENT

Man must be disappointed with the lesser things of life before he can comprehend the full value of the greater. *Bulwer*

We mount to heaven mostly on the ruins of our cherished schemes, finding our failures were successes. *A. B. Alcott*

DUTY

So nigh is grandeur to our dust, so near is God to man, when duty whispers low, "Thou must," the youth replies, "I can." *Emerson*

Do thy duty; that is best; leave unto the Lord the rest.
Longfellow

If I am faithful to the duties of the present, God will provide for the future. *Bedell*

This is the feeling that gives a man true courage—the feeling that he has a work to do at all costs; the sense of duty.
C. Kingsley

Man is not born to solve the problem of the universe, but to find out what he has to do; and to restrain himself within the limits of his comprehension. *Goethe*

EDUCATION

Education does not mean teaching people to know what they do not know; it means teaching them to behave as they do not behave. *Ruskin*

Knowledge does not comprise all which is contained in the large term of education. The feelings are to be disciplined; the passions are to be restrained; true and worthy motives are to be inspired; a profound religious feeling is to be instilled, and pure morality inculcated under all circumstances. All this is comprised in education. *Daniel Webster*

States should spend money and effort on this great all-underlying matter of spiritual education as they have hitherto spent them on beating and destroying each other.
John Galsworthy

ENTHUSIASM

Every great and commanding movement in the annals of the world is the triumph of enthusiasm. Nothing great was ever achieved without it. *Emerson*

The sense of this word among the Greeks affords the noblest definition of it; enthusiasm signifies "God in us."
Mad. De Stael

Every production of genius must be the production of enthusiasm. *Disraeli*

ENVY

If we did but know how little some enjoy of the great things that they possess, there would not be much envy in the world.

Young

The truest mark of being born with great qualities, is being born without envy. *Rochefoucauld*

Envy, like the worm, never runs but to the fairest fruit; like a cunning bloodhound, it singles out the fattest deer in the flock. Abraham's riches were the Philistines' envy, and Jacob's blessings had Esau's hatred. *Beaumont*

Envy always implies conscious inferiority wherever it resides.

Pliny

If envy, like anger, did not burn itself in its own fire, and consume and destroy those persons it possesses before it can destroy those it wishes worst to, it would set the whole world on fire, and leave the most excellent persons the most miserable.

Clarendon

ETERNITY

No man can pass into eternity, for he is already in it.

Farrar

The wish falls often, warm upon my heart, that I may learn nothing here that I cannot continue in the other world; that I may do nothing here but deeds that will bear fruit in heaven.

Richter

The sum and substance of the preparation needed for a coming eternity is, that we believe what the Bible tells us, and do what the Bible bids us. *Chalmers*

The grand difficulty is so to feel the reality of both worlds as to give each its due place in our thoughts and feelings—to keep our mind's eye, and our heart's eye, ever fixed on the land of Promise, without looking away from the road along which we are to travel toward it. *Hare*

EVILS

To be free from evil thoughts is God's best gift. *Aeschylus*

If you do what you should not, you must bear what you would not. *Franklin*

Never let a man imagine that he can pursue a good end by evil means, without sinning against his own soul.—The evil effect on himself is certain. *Southey*

As surely as God is good, so surely there is no such thing as necessary evil. *Southey*

EXAMPLE

There is a transcendent power in example. We reform others unconsciously, when we walk uprightly. *Mad. Swetchine*

Example is more forcible than precept. People look at my six days in the week to see what I mean on the seventh. *Cecil*

The first great gift we can bestow on others is a good example. *Morell*

No man is so insignificant as to be sure his example can do no hurt. *Lord Clarendon*

Of all commentaries upon the Scriptures, good examples are the best and the liveliest. *Donne*

Whatever parent gives his children good instruction, and sets them at the same time a bad example, may be considered as bringing them food in one hand, and poison in the other. *Balguy*

EXPERIENCE

Experience is the name men give to their follies or their sorrows. *Musset*

Experience is the Lord's school, and they who are taught by Him usually learn by the mistakes they make that in themselves they have no wisdom; and by their slips and falls, that they have no strength. *John Newton*

When I was young I was sure of everything; in a few years, having been mistaken a thousand times, I was not half so sure of most things as I was before; at present, I am hardly sure of anything but what God has revealed to me. *John Wesley*

He hazardeth much who depends for his learning on experience. An unhappy master is he who is made wise only by many shipwrecks; a miserable merchant, who is neither rich nor wise till he has been bankrupt. By experience we find out a short way by long wandering. *Roger Ascham*

FAITH

Faith marches at the head of the army of progress. It is found beside the most refined life, the freest government, the profoundest philosophy, the noblest poetry, the purest humanity. *T. T. Munger*

In actual life every great enterprise begins with and takes its first forward step in faith. *Schlegel*

When men cease to be faithful to their God, he who expects to find them so to each other will be much disappointed. *Bp. Horne*

All I have seen teaches me to trust the Creator for all I have not seen. *Emerson*

It is faith among men that holds the moral elements of society together, as it is faith in God that binds the world to his throne. *W. M. Evarts*

Faith does nothing alone—nothing of itself, but everything under God, by God, through God. *Stoughton*

FALSEHOOD

Dare to be true; nothing can need a lie. *Herbert*

None but cowards lie. *Murphy*

He who tells a lie is not sensible how great a task he undertakes; for he must invent twenty more to maintain that one. *Pope*

This above all; to thine own self be true; and it must follow, as the night the day, thou canst not then be false to any man.
Shakespeare

FAME

Fame, to the ambitious, is like salt water to the thirsty—the more one gets, the more he wants. *Ebers*

It often happens that those of whom we speak least on earth are best known in heaven. *Caussin*

Worldly fame is but a breath of wind that blows now this way, and now that, and changes name as it changes direction.
Dante

Time has a doomsday book, on whose pages he is continually recording illustrious names. But as often as a new name is written there, an old one disappears. Only a few stand in illuminated characters never to be effaced. *Longfellow*

FORGIVENESS

To err is human; to forgive, divine. *Pope*

His heart was as great as the world, but there was no room in it to hold the memory of a wrong. *Emerson*

Said General Oglethorpe to Wesley, "I never forgive." "Then I hope, sir," said Wesley, "you never sin."

We hand folks over to God's mercy, and show none ourselves. *George Eliot*

A more glorious victory cannot be gained over another man, than this, that when the injury began on his part, the kindness should begin on ours. *Tillotson*

Humanity is never so beautiful as when praying for forgiveness, or else forgiving another. *Richter*

"I can forgive, but I cannot forget," is only another way of saying, "I will not forgive." Forgiveness ought to be like a cancelled note—torn in two, and burned up, so that it never can be shown against one. *H. W. Beecher*

It is in vain for you to expect, it is impudent for you to ask of God forgiveness for yourself if you refuse to exercise this forgiving temper as to others. *Hoadly*

Forgive many things in others; nothing in yourself. *Ausonius*

FREEDOM

No man is free who is not master of himself. *Epictetus*

This is what I call the American idea of freedom—a government of all the people, by all the people, for all the people; of course, a government of the principles of eternal justice—the unchanging law of God. *Theodore Parker*

FRIENDSHIP

In poverty and other misfortunes of life, true friends are a sure refuge. The young they keep out of mischief; to the old they are a comfort and aid in their weakness, and those in the prime of life they incite to noble deeds. *Aristotle*

All men have their frailties; and whoever looks for a friend without imperfections, will never find what he seeks. We love ourselves notwithstanding our faults, and we ought to love our friends in like manner. *Cyrus*

We take care of our health, we lay up money, we make our roof tight and our clothing sufficient, but who provides wisely that he shall not be wanting in the best property of all—friends? *Emerson*

Life is to be fortified by many friendships.—To love and to be loved is the greatest happiness of existence. *Sydney Smith*

Two persons cannot long be friends if they cannot forgive each other's little failings. *Bruyere*

The only way to have a friend is to be one. *Emerson*

GENEROSITY

He that gives all, though but little, gives much; because God looks not to the quantity of the gift, but to the quality of the givers. *Quarles*

What I gave, I have; what I spent, I had; what I kept, I lost.
Old Epitaph

When you give, take to yourself no credit for generosity, unless you deny yourself something in order that you may give.
H. Taylor

I would have a man generous to his country, his neighbors, his kindred, his friends, and most of all his poor friends. Not like some who are most lavish with those who are able to give most to them. *Pliny*

GOD

I cannot conceive how a man could look up into the heavens and say there is no God. *Abraham Lincoln*

God governs the world, and we have only to do our duty wisely, and leave the issue to him. *John Jay*

How often we look upon God as our last and feeblest resource! We go to him because we have nowhere else to go. And then we learn that the storms of life have driven us, not upon the rocks, but into the desired haven.
George Macdonald

We cannot too often think, that there is a never sleeping eye that reads the heart, and registers our thoughts. *Bacon*

Live near to God, and so all things will appear to you little in comparison with eternal realities. *R. M. McCheyne*

GOODNESS

The best portion of a good man's life is his little, nameless, unremembered acts of kindness and of love. *Wordsworth*

Nothing can make a man truly great but being truly good and partaking of God's holiness. *M. Henry*

How far that little candle throws his beams! so shines a good deed in a naughty world. *Shakespeare*

Goodness consists not in the outward things we do, but in the inward thing we are. To be good is the great thing.
E. H. Chapin

GRATITUDE

He enjoys much who is thankful for little; a grateful mind is both a great and a happy mind. *Secker*

He who receives a benefit should never forget it; he who bestows should never remember it. *Charron*

When I find a great deal of gratitude in a poor man, I take it for granted there would be as much generosity if he were rich. *Pope*

From David learn to give thanks for everything. Every furrow in the Book of Psalms is sown with the seeds of thanksgiving. *Jeremy Taylor*

If gratitude is due from children to their earthly parent, how much more is the gratitude of the great family of men due to our Father in heaven. *H. Ballou*

GREATNESS

No man has come to true greatness who has not felt in some degree that his life belongs to his race, and that what God gives him he gives him for mankind. *Phillips Brooks*

What millions died that Caesar might be great. *Campbell*

He who comes up to his own idea of greatness, must always have had a very low standard of it in his mind. *Ruskin*

The man who does his work, any work, conscientiously, must always be in one sense a great man. *Mulock*

HABIT

Any act often repeated soon forms a habit; and habit allowed, steadily gains in strength. At first it may be but as the spider's web, easily broken through, but if not resisted it soon binds us with chains of steel. *Tryon Edwards*

Habit is a cable. We weave a thread of it every day, and at last we cannot break it. *H. Mann*

Habit is either the best of servants, or the worst of masters. *Emmons*

Sow an act, and you reap a habit; sow a habit, and you reap a character; sow a character, and you reap a destiny.

G. D. Boardman

HAPPINESS

Happiness is neither within us only, or without us; it is the union of ourselves with God. *Pascal*

Call no man happy till you know the end of his life. Till then, at most, he can only be counted fortunate. *Herodotus*

Happiness is not the end of life; character is.

H. W. Beecher

Unhappy is the man who is not so much dissatisfied with what he has as with what the other fellow possesses.

Chauncey M. Depew

An act of goodness is of itself an act of happiness. No reward coming after the event can compare with the sweet reward that went with it. *Maurice Maeterlinck*

To be happy is not the purpose of our being, but to deserve happiness. *Fichte*

HEART

A loving heart is the truest wisdom. *Dickens*

The hardest trial of the heart is whether it can bear a rival's failure without triumph. *Aikin*

The heart of a good man is the sanctuary of God in this world. *Mad. Neckar*

HEAVEN

He that studies to know duty, and labors in all things to do it, will have two heavens—one of joy, peace, and comfort on earth, and the other of glory and happiness beyond the grave.

There is a land where everlasting suns shed everlasting brightness; where the soul drinks from the living streams of love that roll by God's high throne! myriads of glorious ones bring their accepted offering. Oh! how blest to look from this dark prison to that shrine, to inhale one breath of Paradise divine, and enter into that eternal rest which waits the sons of God! *Bowring*

One sweetly solemn thought comes to me o'er and o'er; I'm nearer to my home today than I've ever been before; nearer my Father's house, where the many mansions be; nearer the great white throne, nearer the jasper sea; nearer the bound of life, where I lay my burden down; nearer leaving my cross; nearer wearing my crown! *Phoebe Cary*

Earth has no sorrow that heaven cannot heal. *Moore*

Who seeks for heaven alone to save his soul may keep the path, but will not reach the goal; while he who walks in love may wander far, yet God will bring him where the blessed are.
Henry Van Dyke

HOME

Our home joys are the most delightful earth affords, and the joy of parents in their children is the most holy joy of humanity. It makes their hearts pure and good, it lifts men up to their Father in heaven. *Pestalozzi*

It was the policy of the good old gentleman to make his children feel that home was the happiest place in the world; and I value this delicious homefeeling as one of the choicest gifts a parent can bestow. *Washington Irving*

The most essential element in any home is God.
Dr. Frank Crane

Christianity begins at home. We build our characters there, and what we become in after years is largely determined by our training and home environment. *Tillman Hobson*

Every house where love abides and friendship is a guest, is surely home, and home, sweet home; for there the heart can rest. *Henry Van Dyke*

A dining room table with children's eager, hungry faces around it, ceases to be a mere dining room table, and becomes an altar. *Simeon Strunsky*

HONESTY

Make yourself an honest man, and then you may be sure there is one rascal less in the world. *Carlyle*

God looks only to the pure, not to the full hands. *Laberius*

True honesty takes into account the claims of God as well as those of man; it renders to God the things that are God's, as well as to man the things that are man's. *C. Simmons*

If he does really think that there is no distinction between virtue and vice, when he leaves our houses let us count our spoons. *Johnson*

HOPE

Hope springs eternal in the human breast. *Pope*

Hope is the last thing that dies in man, and though it be exceedingly deceitful, yet it is of this good use to us, that while we are traveling through life it conducts us in an easier and more pleasant way to our journey's end. *Rochefoucauld*

Eternity is the divine treasure house, and hope is the window, by means of which mortals are permitted to see, as through a glass darkly, the things which God is preparing. *Mountford*

My country owes me nothing. It gave me, as it gives every boy and girl, a chance. It gave me schooling, independence of action, opportunity for service and honor. In no other land could a boy from a country village, without inheritance or influential friends, look forward with unbounded hope. *Herbert Hoover*

HUMILITY

It is easy to look down on others; to look down on ourselves is the difficulty. *Peterborough*

Humility is the genuine proof of Christian virtue. Without it we keep all our defects; and they are only crusted over by pride, which conceals them from others, and often from ourselves. *Rochefoucauld*

Heaven's gates are not so highly arched as princes' palaces; they that enter there must go upon their knees. *J. Webster*

It is no great thing to be humble when you are brought low; but to be humble when you are praised is a great and rare attainment. *St. Bernard*

The Christian is like the ripening corn; the riper he grows the more lowly he bends his head. *Guthrie*

I believe the first test of a truly great man is his humility. *Ruskin*

God walks with the humble; He reveals himself to the lowly; He gives understanding to the little ones; He discloses His meaning to pure minds, but hides His grace from the curious and the proud. *Thos. a Kempis*

The fullest and best ears of corn hang lowest toward the ground. *Bp. Reynolds*

IMMORTALITY

The seed dies into a new life, and so does man. *G. Macdonald*

Seems it strange that thou shouldst live forever? Is it less strange that thou shouldst live at all? This is a miracle; and that no more. *Young*

One short sleep past, we wake eternally, and death shall be no more. *Donne*

It is immortality, and that alone, which amid life's pains, abasements, the soul can comfort, elevate, and fill. *Young*

INGRATITUDE

We can be thankful to a friend for a few acres, or a little money; and yet for the freedom and command of the whole earth, and for the great benefits of our being, our life, health, and reason, we look upon ourselves as under no obligation. *Seneca*

What unthankfulness is it to forget our consolations, and to look upon matters of grievance; to think so much upon two or three crosses as to forget an hundred blessings. *Sibbs*

KINDNESS

I expect to pass through life but once. If therefore, there be any kindness I can show, or any good thing I can do to any fellow-being, let me do it now, and not defer or neglect it, as I shall not pass this way again. *Penn*

The best portion of a good man's life is his little, nameless, unremembered acts of kindness and of love. *Wordsworth*

When death, the great reconciler, has come, it is never our tenderness that we repent of, but our severity. *George Eliot*

What do we live for, if it is not to make life less difficult to each other? *George Eliot*

KNOWLEDGE

The first step to knowledge is to know that we are ignorant. *Cecil*

The end of all learning is to know God, and out of that knowledge to love and imitate him. *Milton*

The brightest blaze of intelligence is of incalculably less value than the smallest spark of charity. *W. Nevins*

LIBERTY

Give me the liberty to know, to think, to believe, and to utter freely, according to conscience, above all other liberties. *Milton*

Perfect conformity to the will of God is the sole sovereign and complete liberty. *D'Aubigne*

Christianity is the companion of liberty in all its conflicts, the cradle of its infancy, and the divine source of its claims. *De Tocqueville*

A Bible and a newspaper in every house, a good school in every district,—all studied and appreciated as they merit,—are the principal support of virtue, morality, and civil liberty.
Franklin

LIFE

A little work, a little sleep, a little love and it is all over.
Mary Roberts Rinehart

The idea shared by many that life is a vale of tears is just as false as the idea shared by the great majority, the idea to which youth and health and riches incline you, that life is a place of entertainment. *Tolstoi*

Life is a long lesson in humility. *James M. Barrie*

A useless life is only an early death. *Goethe*

I would so live as if I knew that I received my being only for the benefit of others. *Seneca*

Life is the childhood of our immortality. *Goethe*

I count all that part of my life lost which I spent not in communion with God, or in doing good. *Donne*

Be such a man, and live such a life, that if every man were such as you, and every life a life like yours, this earth would be God's Paradise. *Phillips Brooks*

LOVE

The heart of him who truly loves is a paradise on earth; he has God in himself, for God is love. *Damennais*

We are shaped and fashioned by what we love. *Goethe*

The greatest happiness of life is the conviction that we are loved, loved for ourselves, or rather loved in spite of ourselves.
Hugo

Where there is room in the heart, there is always room in the house. *Moore*

He that careth for the sick and wounded
Watcheth not alone;

There are three in the darkness together
And the third is the Lord.

Henry Van Dyke

The true measure of loving God is to love Him without measure. *St. Bernard*

MAN

A man's ledger does not tell what he is, or what he is worth. —Count what is in man, not what is on him, if you would know what he is worth—whether rich or poor.

H. W. Beecher

It is not what he has, or even what he does which expresses the worth of a man, but what he is. *Amiel*

The older I grow—and I now stand on the brink of eternity —the more comes back to me that sentence in the Catechism which I learned when a child, and the fuller and deeper its meaning becomes: "What is the chief end of man? To glorify God and enjoy him forever." *Carlyle*

Let each man think himself an act of God; his mind a thought, his life a breath of God. *Bailey*

MARRIAGE

I chose my wife, as she did her wedding gown, for qualities that would wear well. *Goldsmith*

Save the love we pay to heaven, there is none purer, holier, than that a virtuous woman feels for him she would cleave to through life. Sisters part from sisters, brothers from brothers, children from their parents, but such a woman from the husband of her choice, never! *Knowles*

The sanctity of marriage and the family relation make the cornerstone of our American society and civilization.

Garfield

What greater thing is there for two human souls than to feel that they are joined for life—to strengthen each other in all labor, to rest on each other in all sorrow, to minister to each

other in all pain, to be one with each other in silent, unspeakable memories at the moment of the last parting.
George Eliot

MERCY

Who will not mercy unto others show, how can he mercy ever hope to have? *Spenser*

Teach me to feel another's woe, to hide the fault I see; that mercy I to others show, that mercy show to me. *Pope*

MISFORTUNE

Our bravest and best lessons are not learned through success, but through misadventure. *A. B. Alcott*

Misfortune is never mournful to the soul that accepts it; for such do always see that in every cloud is an angel's face.
Jerome

Little minds are tamed and subdued by misfortune; but great minds rise above it. *Washington Irving*

MONEY

Money is a good servant, but a poor master. *D. Bouhours*

By doing good with his money, a man, as it were, stamps the image of God upon it, and makes it pass current for the merchandise of heaven. *J. Rutledge*

All our money has a moral stamp. It is coined over again in an inward mint. The uses we put it to, the spirit in which we spend it, give it a character which is plainly perceptible to the eye of God. *T. Starr King*

MOTHER

Children, look in those eyes, listen to that dear voice, notice the feeling of even a single touch that is bestowed upon you by that gentle hand! Make much of it while yet you have that most precious of all good gifts, a loving mother. Read the unfathomable love of those eyes; the kind anxiety of that tone and look, however slight your pain. In after life you may have friends, fond, dear friends, but never will you have again the inexpressible love and gentleness lavished upon you, which none but a mother bestows. *Macaulay*

If you would reform the world from its errors and vices, begin by enlisting the mothers. *C. Simmons*

All that I am, or hope to be, I owe to my angel mother. *Lincoln*

My mother's influence in molding my character was conspicuous. She forced me to learn daily long chapters of the Bible by heart. To that discipline and patient, accurate resolve I owe not only much of my general power of taking pains, but the best part of my taste for literature. *Ruskin*

A man never sees all that his mother has been to him till it's too late to let her know that he sees it. *W. D. Howells*

MUSIC

Next to theology I give to music the highest place and honor. And we see how David and all the saints have wrought their godly thoughts into verse, rhyme, and song. *Luther*

Music is well said to be the speech of angels. *Carlyle*

The meaning of song goes deep. Who is there that, in logical words, can express the effect music has on us? A kind of inarticulate, unfathomable speech, which leads us to the edge of the infinite, and lets us for moments gaze into that! *Carlyle*

NATURE

Looks through nature up to nature's God. *Pope*

There is a signature of wisdom and power impressed on the works of God, which evidently distinguishes them from the feeble imitations of men. Not only the splendor of the sun, but the glimmering light of the glowworm, proclaims his glory. *John Newton*

Nature is the living, visible garment of God. *Goethe*

In contemplation of created things, by steps we may ascend to God. *Milton*

NECESSITY

When God would educate a man He compels him to learn bitter lessons. He sends him to school to the necessities rather than to the graces, that, by knowing all suffering, he may know also the eternal consolation. *Celia Burleigh*

OBEDIENCE

The first law that ever God gave to man, was a law of obedience; it was a commandment pure and simple, wherein man had nothing to inquire after or to dispute, for as much as to obey is the proper office of a rational soul acknowledging a heavenly superior and benefactor. From obedience and submission spring all other virtues, as all sin does from self-opinion and self-will. *Montaigne*

OPPORTUNITY

Next to knowing when to seize an opportunity, the most important thing in life is to know when to forego an advantage. *Disraeli*

There are no times in life when opportunity, the chance to be and do, gathers so richly about the soul as when it has to suffer. Then everything depends on whether the man turns to the lower or the higher helps. If he resorts to mere expedients and tricks the opportunity is lost. He comes out no richer nor greater; nay, he comes out harder, poorer, smaller for his pain. But, if he turns to God, the hour of suffering is the turning hour of his life. *Phillips Brooks*

You will never "find" time for anything. If you want time, you must make it. *Charles Buxton*

Many do with opportunities as children do at the seashore; they fill their little hands with sand, and then let the grains fall through, one by one, till all are gone. *T. Jones*

PARENTS

We never know the love of the parent till we become parents ourselves. When we first bend over the cradle of our own child, God throws back the temple door, and reveals to us the sacredness and mystery of a father's and a mother's love to ourselves. And in later years, when they have gone from us, there is always a certain sorrow, that we cannot tell them we have found it out. One of the deepest experiences of a noble nature in reference to the loved ones that have passed beyond this world, is the thought of what he might have been to them, and done for them, if he had known, while they were living, what he has learned since they died. *H. W. Beecher*

Plato seeing a child do mischief in the streets, went forth and corrected his father for it. And this is the pattern of God's judicial proceedings, for he visits the iniquities of the fathers upon the children who imitate them, and the iniquities of the children upon the fathers who countenance and indulge them.

J. Kitchen

PATIENCE

It's easy finding reasons why other folks should be patient.
George Eliot

Our real blessings often appear to us in the shape of pains, losses, and disappointments; but let us have patience, and we soon shall see them in their proper figures. *Addison*

There are times when God asks nothing of his children except silence, patience, and tears. *C. S. Robinson*

PEACE

Peace is the happy, natural state of man; war, his corruption, his disgrace. *Thomson*

There are interests by the sacrifice of which peace is too dearly purchased. One should never be at peace to the shame of his own soul, to the violation of his integrity or of his allegiance to God. *E. H. Chapin*

PLEASURE

Would you judge of the lawfulness or unlawfulness of pleasure, take this rule: whatever weakens your reason, impairs the tenderness of your conscience, obscures your sense of God, or takes off the relish of spiritual things; in short, whatever increases the strength and authority of your body over your mind, that is sin to you, however, innocent it may be in itself.

Southey

The pursuit in which we cannot ask God's protection must be criminal: the pleasure for which we dare not thank him cannot be innocent. *Richard Fuller*

PRAYER

I have been driven many times to my knees by the overwhelming conviction that I had nowhere else to go. My own wisdom, and that of all about me, seemed insufficient for the day. *Abraham Lincoln*

A prayer in its simplest definition is merely a wish turned Godward. *Phillips Brooks*

Trouble and perplexity drive me to prayer, and prayer drives away perplexity and trouble. *Melanchthon*

Practice in life whatever you pray for, and God will give it to you more abundantly. *Pusey*

If you cannot pray over a thing, and cannot ask God to bless you in it, don't do that thing. A secret that you would keep from God is a secret that you should keep from your own heart.

Open thy heart to God, if he be there, the outspread world will be thy book of prayer. *Tholuck*

Let our prayers, like the ancient sacrifices, ascend morning and evening. Let our days begin and end with God.

Channing

The Lord's Prayer is not, as some fancy, the easiest, the most natural of all devout utterances. It may be committed to memory quickly, but it is slowly learned by heart. *Maurice*

The Christian will find his parentheses for prayer even in the busiest hours of life. *Cecil*

PREJUDICE

Prejudice is the child of ignorance. *Hazlitt*

The prejudiced and obstinate man does not so much hold opinions, as his opinions hold him. *Tryon Edwards*

Even when we fancy we have grown wiser, it is only, it may be, that new prejudices have displaced old ones. *Bovee*

PRIDE

The seat of pride is in the heart, and only there; and if it be not there, it is neither in the look, nor in the clothes.
Lord Clarendon

As Plato entertained some friends in a room where there was a couch richly ornamented, Diogenes came in very dirty, as usual, and getting upon the couch, and trampling on it, said, "I trample upon the pride of Plato." Plato mildly answered, "But with greater pride, Diogenes!" *Erasmus*

A proud man is seldom a grateful man, for he never thinks he gets as much as he deserves. *H. W. Beecher*

John Bunyan had a great dread of spiritual pride; and once, after he had preached a very fine sermon, and his friends crowded round to shake him by the hand, while they expressed the utmost admiration of his eloquence, he interrupted them, saying: "Ay! you need not remind me of that, for the Devil told me of it before I was out of the pulpit!" *Southey*

PROSPERITY

Everything in the world may be endured, except continual prosperity. *Goethe*

He that swells in prosperity will be sure to shrink in adversity. *Colton*

One is never more on trial than in the moment of excessive good fortune. *Lew Wallace*

While prosperous you can number many friends; but when the storm comes you are left alone. *Ovid*

PROVIDENCE

Every blade of grass in the field is measured; the green cups and the colored crowns of every flower are curiously counted; the stars of the firmament wheel in cunningly calculated orbits; even the storms have their laws. *Blaikie*

Either all is chance, and being but chance is of no consequence, or God rules the world, and all is well. Whatever befalls is just and right, and therefore not unendurable. *Andrew Lang*

PUNISHMENT

The whole of life and experience goes to show, that right or wrong doing, whether as to the physical or the spiritual nature, is sure in the end to meet its appropriate reward or punishment. Penalties may be delayed but they are sure to come. *H. W. Beecher*

RELIGION

Men will wrangle for religion; write for it; fight for it; die for it; anything but live for it. *Colton*

Religion would not have enemies, if it were not an enemy to their vices. *Massillon*

Measure not men by Sundays, without regarding what they do all the week after. *Fuller*

A life that will bear the inspection of men and of God, is the only certificate of true religion. *Johnson*

REPENTANCE

To do so no more is the truest repentance. *Luther*

There is a greater depravity in not repenting of sin when it has been committed, than in committing it at first. To deny, as Peter did, is bad; but not to weep bitterly, as he did, when we have denied, is worse. *Payson*

Repentance, to be of any avail, must work a change of heart and conduct. *T. L. Cuyler*

Whatever stress some may lay upon it, a death-bed repentance is but a weak and slender plank to trust our all upon. *Sterne*

REPUTATION

Reputation is what men and women think of us; character is what God and angels know of us. *Paine*

RESPONSIBILITY

The most important thought I ever had was that of my individual responsibility to God. *Daniel Webster*

RICHES

To value riches is not to be covetous. They are the gift of God, and, like every gift of his, good in themselves, and capable of a good use. But to overvalue riches, to give them a place in the heart which God did not design them to fill, this is covetousness. *H. L. Wayland*

Riches without charity are nothing worth. They are a blessing only to him who makes them a blessing to others. *Fielding*

In this world, it is not what we take up, but what we give up, that makes us rich. *H. W. Beecher*

Nothing is so hard for those who abound in riches as to conceive how others can be in want. *Swift*

SABBATH

He that remembers not to keep the Christian Sabbath at the beginning of the week, will be in danger of forgetting, before the end of the week, that he is a Christian. *E. Turner*

Without a Sabbath, no worship; without worship, no religion; and without religion, no permanent freedom. *Montalembert*

God's altar stands from Sunday to Sunday, and the seventh day is no more for religion than any other—it is for rest. The whole seven are for religion, and one of them for rest, for instruction, for social worship, for gaining strength for the other six. *H. W. Beecher*

SELFISHNESS

Think about yourself, about what you want, what you like, what respect people ought to pay you, what people think of you, and then to you nothing will be pure. May God keep our hearts pure from that selfishness which is the root of all sin. *C. Kingsley*

SIN

Sin is, essentially, a departure from God. *Luther*

The deadliest sin were the consciousness of no sin. *Carlyle*

No sin is small. It is against an infinite God, and may have consequences immeasurable. No grain of sand is small in the mechanism of a watch. *Jeremy Taylor*

Sins are like circles in the water when a stone is thrown into it; one produces another. When anger was in Cain's heart, murder was not far off. *Philip Henry*

STEWARDSHIP

As to all that we have and are, we are but stewards of the Most High God. On all our possessions, on our time, and talents, and influence, and property, he has written, "Occupy for me, and till I shall come." To obey his instructions and serve him faithfully, is the true test of obedience and discipleship. *C. Simmons*

There is no portion of our time that is our time, and the rest God's; there is no portion of money that is our money, and the rest God's money. It is all His; He made it all, gives it all, and He has simply trusted it to us for His service. A servant has two purses, the master's and his own, but we have only one. *Monod*

SUCCESS

He that has never known adversity, is but half acquainted with others, or with himself. Constant success shows us but one side of the world. For, as it surrounds us with friends, who will tell us only our merits, so it silences those enemies from whom alone we can learn our defect. *Colton*

Possessions, outward success, publicity, luxury—to me these have always been contemptible. I believe that a simple and unassuming manner of life is best for everyone, best both for the body and the mind. *Albert Einstein*

Character is the real foundation of all worth-while success.
John Hays Hammond

TEARS

There ought to be more tears of penitence over our neglects of Christ, more tears of sympathy with the afflicted, and more tears of joy over the infinite good things which Jesus brings to us. *T. L. Cuyler*

TEMPTATION

Bearing up against temptations and prevailing over them is the very thing wherein the whole life of religion consists. It is the trial which God puts upon us in this world, by which we are to make evidence of our love and obedience to him, and of our fitness to be made members of his kingdom.
Samuel Clarke

To realize God's presence is the one sovereign remedy against temptation. *Fenelon*

THANKFULNESS

God has two dwellings: one in heaven, and the other in a meek and thankful heart. *Izaak Walton*

God's goodness hath been great to thee. Let never day nor night unhallowed pass but still remember what the Lord hath done. *Shakespeare*

Pride slays thanksgiving, but an humble mind is the soil out of which thanks naturally grow. A proud man is seldom a grateful man, for he never thinks he gets as much as he deserves. *H. W. Beecher*

TIME

Time is lent us to be laid out in God's service, and we cannot be too diligent in it, if we consider that time is precious, short, passing, uncertain, irrevocable when gone, and that for which we must be accountable.

There is no saying shocks me so much as that which I hear very often, "that a man does not know how to pass his time." *Cowley*

Lost wealth may be restored by industry, the wreck of health regained by temperance, forgotten knowledge restored by study, alienated friendship smoothed into forgetfulness, even forfeited reputation won by penitence and virtue. But who ever looked upon his vanished hours, recalled his slighted years, stamped them with wisdom, or effaced from Heaven's record the fearful blot of wasted time? *Mrs. Sigourney*

TRIALS

God had one Son on earth without sin, but never one without suffering. *Augustine*

Great trials seem to be a necessary preparation for great duties. *E. Thomson*

There are no crown-wearers in heaven that were not cross-bearers here below. *Spurgeon*

TRIFLES

Trifles make perfection, but perfection itself is no trifle. *Michelangelo*

Johnson well says, "He who waits to do a great deal of good at once will never do anything." Life is made up of little things. It is very rarely that an occasion is offered for doing a great deal at once. True greatness consists in being great in little things. *C. Simmons*

TRUTH

If the world goes against truth, then Athanasius goes against the world. *Athanasius*

To seek for the truth, for the sake of knowing the truth, is one of the noblest objects a man can live for. *Dean Inge*

The greatest friend of truth is time; her greatest enemy is prejudice; and her constant companion is humility. *Colton*

WAR

The greatest curse that can be entailed on mankind is a state of war. All the atrocious crimes committed in years of peace, all that is spent in peace by the secret corruptions, or by the thoughtless extravagance of nations, are mere trifles compared with the gigantic evils which stalk over this world in a state of war. God is forgotten in war; every principle of Christianity is trampled upon. *Sidney Smith*

There never was a good war, or a bad peace. *Franklin*

WORSHIP

A church-going people are apt to be a law-abiding people. *E. A. Park*

What greater calamity can fall upon a nation than the loss of worship. *Carlyle*

YEARNINGS

Tell me what are the prevailing sentiments that occupy the minds of your young men, and I will tell you what is to be the character of the next generation. *Burke*

YOUTH

The destiny of any nation, at any given time, depends on the opinions of its young men under five-and-twenty. *Goethe*

I would not waste my spring of youth in idle dalliance; I would plant rich seeds, to blossom in my manhood, and bear fruit when I am old. *Hillhouse*

Youth, though it may lack knowledge, is certainly not devoid of intelligence; it sees through shams with sharp and terrible eyes. *H. L. Mencken*

CHAPTER VI

QUOTATIONS FROM THE BIBLE

ABILITY

If ye have faith as a grain of mustard seed . . . nothing shall be impossible unto you. *Matt. 17:20*

With men this is impossible; but with God all things are possible. *Matt. 19:26*

All things are possible to him that believeth. *Mark 9:23*

I can do all things through Christ which strengtheneth me. *Phil. 4:13*

ABSENT

The Lord watch between me and thee, when we are absent one from another. *Gen. 31:49*

ACHIEVEMENT

Which of you, intending to build a tower, sitteth not down first, and counteth the cost, whether he have sufficient to finish it? *Luke 14:28*

My meat is to do the will of him that sent me, and to finish his work. *John 4:34*

I have fought a good fight, I have finished my course, I have kept the faith. *2 Tim. 4:7*

AFFLICTION

In my distress I called upon the Lord, and cried to my God; and he did hear my voice out of his temple. *2 Sam. 22:7*

Yea, though I walk through the valley of the shadow of death, I will fear no evil: for thou art with me; thy rod and thy staff they comfort me. *Psa. 23:4*

Cast thy burden upon the Lord, and he shall sustain thee; he shall never suffer the righteous to be moved. *Psa. 55:22*

Come unto me, all ye that labour and are heavy laden, and I will give you rest. *Matt. 11:28*

O my Father, if it be possible, let this cup pass from me: nevertheless, not as I will, but as thou wilt. *Matt. 26:39*

Who shall separate us from the love of Christ? shall tribulation, or distress, or persecution? *Rom. 8:35*

Bear ye one another's burdens, and so fulfil the law of Christ. *Gal. 6:2*

Endure hardness, as a good soldier of Jesus Christ. *2 Tim. 2:3*

If we suffer, we shall also reign with him. *2 Tim. 2:12*

The Lord is my helper, and I will not fear what man shall do unto me. *Heb. 13:6*

AMBITION

Labour not to be rich . . . Wilt thou set thine eyes upon that which is not? for riches certainly make themselves wings; they fly away as an eagle toward heaven. *Prov. 23:4, 5*

What is a man profited, if he shall gain the whole world, and lose his own soul? *Matt. 16:26*

He that is greatest among you shall be your servant. And whosoever shall exalt himself shall be abased; and he that shall humble himself shall be exalted. *Matt. 23:11, 12*

ANGER

He that is slow to anger is better than the mighty; and he that ruleth his spirit than he that taketh a city. *Prov. 16:32*

Be not hasty in thy spirit to be angry: for anger resteth in the bosom of fools. *Eccl. 7:9*

ANXIETY

Yea, though I walk through the valley of the shadow of death, I will fear no evil: for thou art with me; thy rod and thy staff they comfort me. *Psa. 23:4*

Behold, God is my salvation: I will trust, and not be afraid. *Isa. 12:2*

Take no thought for your life, what ye shall eat, or what ye shall drink; nor yet for your body, what ye shall put on. Is not the life more than meat, and the body than raiment? *Matt. 6:25*

Let not your heart be troubled: ye believe in God, believe also in me. *John 14:1*

Peace I leave with you, my peace I give unto you: not as the world giveth, give I unto you. Let not your heart be troubled, neither let it be afraid. *John 14:27*

Perfect love casteth out fear. *1 John 4:18*

APPEARANCE

Man looketh on the outward appearance, but the Lord looketh on the heart. *1 Sam. 16:7*

Judge not according to the appearance. *John 7:24*

GREED

Thou shalt not covet thy neighbour's house, thou shalt not covet thy neighbour's wife, nor his manservant, nor his maidservant, nor his ox, nor his ass, nor any thing that is thy neighbour's. *Ex. 20:17*

From the least of them even unto the greatest of them every one is given to covetousness. *Jer. 6:13*

Take heed, and beware of covetousness: for a man's life consisteth not in the abundance of the things which he possesseth. *Luke 12:15*

The love of money is the root of all evil. *1 Tim. 6:10*

BAPTISM

Go ye therefore, and teach all nations, baptizing them in the name of the Father, and of the Son, and of the Holy Ghost. *Matt. 28:19*

He that believeth and is baptized shall be saved.
Mark 16:16

Except a man be born of water and of the Spirit, he cannot enter into the kingdom of God. *John 3:5*

Repent, and be baptized every one of you in the name of Jesus Christ for the remission of sins. *Acts 2:38*

BEHAVIOR

Walk in the fear of our God. *Neh. 5:9*

Walk in the way of good men, and keep the paths of righteousness. *Prov. 2:20*

Whatsoever ye would that men should do to you, do ye even so to them. *Matt. 7:12*

Whether . . . ye eat, or drink, or whatsoever ye do, do all to the glory of God. *1 Cor. 10:31*

Be thou an example of the believers, in word, in conversation, in charity, in spirit, in faith, in purity. *1 Tim. 4:12*

BENEDICTION

The Lord watch between me and thee, when we are absent one from another. *Gen. 31:49*

The Lord bless thee, and keep thee: The Lord make his face shine upon thee, and be gracious unto thee: The Lord lift up his countenance upon thee, and give thee peace.
Num. 6:24-26

Grace be unto you, and peace, from God our Father, and from the Lord Jesus Christ. *1 Cor. 1:3*

The grace of the Lord Jesus Christ, and the love of God, and the communion of the Holy Ghost, be with you all.
2 Cor. 13:14

Now the God of peace, that brought again from the dead our Lord Jesus, that great shepherd of the sheep, through the blood of the everlasting covenant, Make you perfect in every good work to do his will, working in you that which is well-pleasing in his sight, through Jesus Christ; to whom be glory for ever and ever. Amen. *Heb. 13:20, 21*

BLESSED

Blessed are all they that put their trust in him. *Psa. 2:12*

Blessed is he whose transgression is forgiven, whose sin is covered. *Psa. 32:1*

Blessed is the man that maketh the Lord his trust. *Psa. 40:4*

Blessed is the man that feareth the Lord, that delighteth greatly in his commandments. *Psa. 112:1*

Blessed are they that hear the word of God, and keep it. *Luke 11:28*

Blessed are they that do his commandments. *Rom. 22:14*

BOASTING

Talk no more so exceeding proudly; let no arrogancy come out of your mouth: for the Lord is a God of knowledge, and by him actions are weighed. *1 Sam. 2:3*

Most men will proclaim every one his own goodness; but a faithful man who can find? *Prov. 20:6*

Boast not thyself of tomorrow; for thou knowest not what a day may bring forth. *Prov. 27:1*

Let another man praise thee, and not thine own mouth; a stranger, and not thine own lips. *Prov. 27:2*

BODY

Dust thou art, and unto dust shalt thou return. *Gen. 3:19*

Take no thought of your life, what ye shall eat, or what ye shall drink; nor yet for your body, what ye shall put on. Is not the life more than meat, and the body than raiment? *Matt. 6:25*

BROTHERHOOD

Let there be no strife, I pray thee, between me and thee . . . for we be brethren. *Gen. 13:8*

A friend loveth at all times, and a brother is born for adversity.
Prov. 17:17

Have we not all one father? Hath not one God created us?
Mal. 2:10

One is your Master, even Christ; and all ye are brethren.
Matt. 23:8

A new commandment I give unto you, That ye love one another; as I have loved you, that ye also love one another.
John 13:34

He that loveth not his brother abideth in death.
1 John 3:14

CHARITY

As ye would that men should do to you, do ye also to them likewise.
Luke 6:31

Though I speak with the tongues of men and of angels, and have not charity, I am become as sounding brass, or a tinkling cymbal. And though I have the gift of prophecy, and understand all mysteries, and all knowledge; and though I have all faith, so that I could remove mountains, and have not charity, I am nothing. And though I bestow all my goods to feed the poor, and though I give my body to be burned, and have not charity, it profiteth me nothing.

Charity suffereth long, and is kind; charity envieth not; charity vaunteth not itself, is not puffed up, Doth not behave itself unseemly, seeketh not her own, is not easily provoked, thinketh no evil; Rejoiceth not in iniquity, but rejoiceth in the truth; Beareth all things, believeth all things, hopeth all things, endureth all things.
1 Cor. 13:1-7

And now abideth faith, hope, charity, these three; but the greatest of these is charity.
Cor. 13:13

Be ye kind one to another, tenderhearted, forgiving one another, even as God for Christ's sake hath forgiven you.
Eph. 4:32

CHILDREN

Train up a child in the way he should go: and when he is old, he will not depart from it. *Prov. 22:6*

Except ye be converted, and become as little children, ye shall not enter into the kingdom of heaven. *Matt. 18:3*

Suffer little children, and forbid them not, to come unto me: for of such is the kingdom of heaven. *Matt. 19:14*

When I was a child, I spake as a child, I understood as a child, I thought as a child: but when I became a man, I put away childish things. *1 Cor. 13:11*

CHRIST

The Son of man came not to be ministered unto, but to minister, and to give his life a ransom for many. *Matt. 20:28*

The Son of man hath power on earth to forgive sins. *Mark 2:10*

I am the bread of life; he that cometh to me shall never hunger; and he that believeth on me shall never thirst. *John 6:35*

I am the door: by me if any man enter in, he shall be saved. *John 10:9*

I am the way, the truth, and the life. *John 14:6*

CHURCH

Mine house shall be called a house of prayer for all people. *Isa. 56:7*

Ye are all the children of God by faith in Christ Jesus. *Gal. 3:26*

The church is subject unto Christ. *Eph. 5:24*

He is the head of the body, the church. *Col. 1:18*

CONVERSION

If the wicked will turn from all his sins that he hath committed, and keep all my statutes, and do that which is lawful and right, he shall surely live, he shall not die. *Ezek. 18:21*

Except ye be converted, and become as little children, ye shall not enter into the kingdom of heaven. *Matt. 18:3*

I will arise and go to my father, and will say unto him, Father, I have sinned against heaven, and before thee. *Luke 15:18*

Behold, I stand at the door and knock: if any man hear my voice, and open the door, I will come in to him, and will sup with him, and he with me. *Rev. 3:20*

COURAGE

Yea, though I walk through the valley of the shadow of death, I will fear no evil: for thou art with me; thy rod and thy staff they comfort me. *Psa. 23:4*

The Lord is my light and my salvation; whom shall I fear? the Lord is the strength of my life; of whom shall I be afraid? *Psa. 27:1*

Be of good courage, and he shall strengthen your heart, all ye that hope in the Lord. *Psa. 31:24*

I sought the Lord, and he heard me, and delivered me from all my fears. *Psa. 34:4*

What time I am afraid, I will trust in thee. *Psa. 56:3*

DEATH

Dust thou art, and unto dust shalt thou return. *Gen. 3:19*

Let me die the death of the righteous, and let my last end be like his! *Num. 23:10*

There the wicked cease from troubling; and there the weary be at rest. There the prisoners rest together; they hear not the voice of the oppressor. The small and great are there; and the servant is free from his master. *Job 3:17-19*

Yea, though I walk through the valley of the shadow of death, I will fear no evil: for thou art with me; thy rod and thy staff they comfort me. *Psa. 23:4*

I must work the works of him that sent me, while it is day: the night cometh, when no man can work. *John 9:4*

O death, where is thy sting? O grave, where is thy victory? *1 Cor. 15:55*

We know that if our earthly house of this tabernacle were dissolved, we have a building of God, an house not made with hands, eternal in the heavens. *2 Cor. 5:1*

We brought nothing into this world, and it is certain we can carry nothing out. *1 Tim. 6:7*

God shall wipe away all tears from their eyes; and there shall be no more death, neither sorrow, nor crying, neither shall there be any more pain: for the former things are passed away. *Rev. 21:4*

DISCOURAGED

Fear not, neither be discouraged. *Deut. 1:21*

When my soul fainted within me I remembered the Lord. *Jonah 2:7*

DUTY

What doth the Lord require of thee, but to do justly, and to love mercy, and to walk humbly with thy God? *Mic. 6:8*

Wist ye not that I must be about my Father's business? *Luke 2:49*

Render therefore unto Caesar the things which be Caesar's, and unto God the things which be God's. *Luke 20:25*

ENMITY

Rejoice not when thine enemy falleth, and let not thine heart be glad when he stumbleth. *Prov. 24:17*

Love your enemies, bless them that curse you, do good to them that hate you, and pray for them which despitefully use you, and persecute you. *Matt. 5:44*

If ye forgive men their trespasses, your heavenly Father will also forgive you. *Matt. 6:14*

If thine enemy hunger, feed him; if he thirst, give him drink; for in so doing thou shalt heap coals of fire on his head.
Rom. 12:20

ENVY

Jealousy is cruel as the grave: the coals thereof are coals of fire, which hath a most vehement flame. *S. of S. 8:6*

Charity envieth not. *1 Cor. 13:4*

Let us not be desirous of vain glory, provoking one another, envying one another. *Gal. 5:26*

ETERNITY

The eternal God is thy refuge, and underneath are the everlasting arms. *Deut. 33:27*

The Lord shall endure for ever. *Psa. 9:7*

Before the mountains were brought forth, or ever thou hadst formed the earth and the world, even from everlasting to everlasting, thou art God. *Psa. 90:2*

For thine is the kingdom, and the power, and the glory, for ever. *Matt. 6:13*

EVIL

It is a sport to a fool to do mischief: but a man of understanding hath wisdom. *Prov. 10:23*

The way of the wicked is an abomination unto the Lord: but he loveth him that followeth after righteousness.
Prov. 15:9

As he thinketh in his heart, so is he. *Prov. 23:7*

There is no peace, saith my God, to the wicked. *Isa. 57:21*

A good man out of the good treasure of the heart bringeth forth good things; and an evil man out of the evil treasure bringeth forth evil things. *Matt. 12:35*

Abstain from all appearance of evil. *1 Thess. 5:22*

EXAMPLE

Let your light so shine before men, that they may see your good works, and glorify your Father which is in heaven.
Matt. 5:16

Be ye therefore perfect, even as your Father which is in heaven is perfect. *Matt. 5:48*

Be ye therefore merciful, as your Father also is merciful.
Luke 6:36

I have given you an example, that ye should do as I have done to you. *John 13:15*

Take heed lest by any means this liberty of yours become a stumbling-block to them that are weak. *1 Cor. 8:9*

FAITH

Offer the sacrifices of righteousness, and put your trust in the Lord. *Psa. 4:5*

Commit thy way unto the Lord; trust also in him; and he shall bring it to pass. *Psa. 37:5*

What time I am afraid, I will trust in thee. *Psa. 56:3*

Whoso putteth his trust in the Lord shall be safe.
Prov. 29:25

All things, whatsoever ye shall ask in prayer, believing, ye shall receive. *Matt. 21:22*

If thou canst believe, all things are possible to him that believeth. *Mark 9:23*

By grace are ye saved through faith; and that not of yourselves: it is the gift of God. *Eph. 2:8*

I have fought a good fight, I have finished my course, I have kept the faith. *2 Tim. 4:7*

He that cometh to God must believe that he is, and that he is a rewarder of them that diligently seek him. *Heb. 11:6*

FAITHFULNESS

A friend loveth at all times, and a brother is born for adversity. *Prov. 17:17*

He that is faithful in that which is least is faithful also in much: and he that is unjust in the least is unjust also in much. *Luke 16:10*

Be thou faithful unto death, and I will give thee a crown of life. *Rev. 2:10*

FALSEHOOD

Thou shalt not bear false witness against they neighbour. *Ex. 20:16*

Ye shall not steal, neither deal falsely, neither lie one to another. *Lev. 19:11*

An hypocrite with his mouth destroyeth his neighbour. *Prov. 11:9*

A false witness shall not be unpunished, and he that speaketh lies shall not escape. *Prov. 19:5*

FLATTERY

The poor is hated even of his own neighbour: but the rich hath many friends. *Prov. 14:20*

Many will intreat the favour of the prince: and every man is a friend to him that giveth gifts. *Prov. 19:6*

Woe unto you, when all men shall speak well of you! for so did their fathers to the false prophets. *Luke 6:26*

FOLLY

Every one that heareth these sayings of mine, and doeth them not, shall be likened unto a foolish man, which built his house upon the sand. *Matt. 7:26*

God hath chosen the foolish things of the world to confound the wise. *1 Cor. 1:27*

The wisdom of this world is foolishness with God.
1 Cor. 3:19

FOOL

The fear of the Lord is the beginning of knowledge: but fools despise wisdom and instruction. *Prov. 1:7*

A foolish son is a grief to his father, and bitterness to her that bare him. *Prov. 17:25*

A fool's mouth is his destruction, and his lips are the snare of his soul. *Prov. 18:7*

Answer not a fool according to his folly, lest thou also be like unto him. *Prov. 26:4*

FORGIVENESS

Rejoice not when thine enemy falleth, and let not thine heart be glad when he stumbleth. *Prov. 24:17*

Love your enemies, bless them that curse you, do good to them that hate you, and pray for them which despitefully use you, and persecute you. *Matt. 5:44*

Forgive us our debts, as we forgive our debtors.
Matt. 6:12

If ye forgive men their trespasses, your heavenly Father will also forgive you. *Matt. 6:14*

Why beholdest thou the mote that is in thy brother's eye, but considerest not the beam that is in thine own eye?
Matt. 7:3

When ye stand praying, forgive, if ye have ought against any: that your Father also which is in heaven may forgive you your trespasses. *Mark 11:25*

Judge not, and ye shall not be judged: condemn not, and ye shall not be condemned: forgive, and ye shall be forgiven.
Luke 6:37

Be ye kind one to another, tenderhearted, forgiving one another, even as God for Christ's sake hath forgiven you.
Eph. 4:32

FRIENDSHIP

A friend loveth at all times, and a brother is born for adversity. *Prov. 17:17*

Greater love hath no man than this, that a man lay down his life for his friends. *John 15:13*

GIVING

Blessed is he that considereth the poor: the Lord will deliver him in time of trouble. *Psa. 41:1*

He that hath pity upon the poor lendeth unto the Lord; and that which he hath given will he pay him again.
Prov. 19:17

If thine enemy be hungry, give him bread to eat; and if he be thirsty, give him water to drink. *Prov. 25:21*

Take heed that ye do not your alms before men, to be seen of them. But when thou doest alms, let not thy left hand know what thy right hand doeth. *Matt. 6:1, 3*

Freely ye have received; freely give. *Matt. 10:8*

Inasmuch as ye have done it unto one of the least of these my brethren, ye have done it unto me. *Matt. 25:40*

Though I bestow all my goods to feed the poor, and though I give my body to be burned, and have not charity, it profiteth me nothing. *1 Cor. 13:3*

GOD

The heavens declare the glory of God; and the firmament sheweth his handywork. *Psa. 19:1*

The fool hath said in his heart, There is no God. *Psa. 14:1*

God is our refuge and strength, a very present help in trouble.
Psa. 46:1

Thou, O Lord, art a God full of compassion, and gracious, longsuffering, and plenteous in mercy and truth. *Psa. 86:15*

Thou art my father, my God, and the rock of my salvation. *Psa. 89:26*

The Lord is good; his mercy is everlasting; and his truth endureth to all generations. *Psa. 100:5*

Our Father which art in heaven, Hallowed be thy name. *Matt. 6:9*

Thine is the kingdom, and the power, and the glory, for ever. *Matt. 6:13*

God is no respecter of persons. *Acts 20:34*

GOSSIP

Thou shalt not go up and down as a talebearer among thy people. *Lev. 19:16*

Let none of you suffer as . . . a busybody in other men's matters. *1 Pet. 4:15*

HARVEST

Ye shall know them by their fruits. Do men gather grapes of thorns, or figs of thistles? *Matt. 7:16*

Every good tree bringeth forth good fruit; but a corrupt tree bringeth forth evil fruit. *Matt. 7:17*

Whatsoever a man soweth, that shall he also reap. *Gal. 6:7*

The harvest truly is plenteous, but the labourers are few. *Matt. 9:37*

HATRED

Thou shalt not hate thy brother in thine heart. *Lev. 19:17*

Love your enemies, bless them that curse you, do good to them that hate you, and pray for them which despitefully use you, and persecute you. *Matt. 5:44*

If ye forgive not men their trespasses, neither will your Father forgive your trespasses. *Matt. 6:15*

He that hateth his brother is in darkness, and walketh in darkness, and knoweth not whither he goeth, because that darkness hath blinded his eyes. *1 John 2:11*

Whosoever doeth not righteousness is not of God, neither he that loveth not his brother. *1 John 3:10*

He that loveth not his brother abideth in death.
1 John 3:14

If a man say, I love God, and hateth his brother, he is a liar: for he that loveth not his brother whom he hath seen, how can he love God whom he hath not seen? *1 John 4:20*

HEART

The Lord seeth not as man seeth; for man looketh on the outward appearance, but the Lord looketh on the heart.
Sam. 16:7

Create in me a clean heart, O God; and renew a right spirit within me. *Psa. 51:10*

Blessed are the pure in heart: for they shall see God.
Matt. 5:8

HEAVEN

There the wicked cease from troubling; and there the weary be at rest. *Job 3:17*

Lay up for yourselves treasures in heaven, where neither moth nor rust doth corrupt, and where thieves do not break through nor steal. *Matt. 6:20*

In my Father's house are many mansions. *John 14:2*

Ye have in heaven a better and an enduring substance.
Heb. 10:34

God shall wipe away all tears from their eyes; and there shall be no more death, neither sorrow, nor crying, neither shall there be any more pain: for the former things are passed away.
Rev. 21:4

HOPE

Be of good courage, and he shall strengthen your heart, all ye that hope in the Lord. *Psa. 31:24*

Why art thou cast down, O my soul? and why art thou disquieted within me? hope in God. *Psa. 43:5*

The righteous hath hope in his death. *Prov. 14:32*

Blessed is the man that trusteth in the Lord, and whose hope the Lord is. *Jer. 17:7*

HUMILITY

What doth the Lord require of thee, but to . . . walk humbly with thy God? *Mic. 6:8*

Take my yoke upon you, and learn of me; for I am meek and lowly in heart: and ye shall find rest unto your souls. *Matt. 11:29*

Whosoever therefore shall humble himself as this little child, the same is greatest in the kingdom of heaven. *Matt. 18:4*

Whosoever will be great among you, let him be your minister; And whosoever will be chief among you, let him be your servant. *Matt. 20:26, 27*

Whosoever shall exalt himself shall be abased; and he that shall humble himself shall be exalted. *Matt. 23:12*

God forbid that I should glory, save in the cross of our Lord Jesus Christ. *Gal. 6:14*

HYPOCRISY

When thou doest thine alms, do not sound a trumpet before thee, as the hypocrites do in the synagogues and in the streets, that they may have glory of men. *Matt. 6:2*

No man can serve two masters: for either he will hate the one, and love the other; or else he will hold to the one, and despise the other. Ye cannot serve God and mammon. *Matt. 6:24*

Thou hypocrite, first cast out the beam out of thine own eye; and then shalt thou see clearly to cast out the mote out of thy brother's eye. *Matt. 7:5*

Not every one that saith unto me, Lord, Lord, shall enter into the kingdom of heaven; but he that doeth the will of my Father which is in heaven. *Matt. 7:21*

Woe unto you, scribes and Pharisees, hypocrites! for ye make clean the outside of the cup and of the platter, but within they are full of extortion and excess. *Matt. 23:25*

The Pharisee stood and prayed thus with himself, God, I thank thee, that I am not as other men are. *Luke 18:11*

If a man say, I love God, and hateth his brother, he is a liar. *1 John 4:20*

IDLENESS

He becometh poor that dealeth with a slack hand: but the hand of the diligent maketh rich. *Prov. 10:4*

The sluggard will not plow by reason of the cold; therefore shall he beg in harvest, and have nothing. *Prov. 20:4*

Drowsiness shall clothe a man with rags. *Prov. 23:21*

IGNORANCE

Fools despise wisdom and instruction. *Prov. 1:7*

Folly is joy to him that is destitute of wisdom: but a man of understanding walketh uprightly. *Prov. 15:21*

Then said Jesus, Father, forgive them; for they know not what they do. *Luke 23:34*

Eye hath not seen, nor ear heard, neither have entered into the heart of man, the things which God hath prepared for them that love him. *1 Cor. 2:9*

IMMORTALITY

For God so loved the world, that he gave his only begotten Son, that whosoever believeth in him should not perish, but have everlasting life. *John 3:16*

I am the resurrection, and the life: he that believeth in me, though he were dead, yet shall he live: And whosoever liveth and believeth in me shall never die. *John 11:25, 26*

The gift of God is eternal life through Jesus Christ our Lord. *Rom. 6:23*

O death, where is thy sting? O grave, where is thy victory? *1 Cor. 15:55*

The world passeth away, and the lust thereof: but he that doeth the will of God abideth for ever. *1 John 2:17*

INDECISION

How long halt ye between two opinions? if the Lord be God, follow him; but if Baal, then follow him. *1 Kin. 18:21*

No man can serve two masters: for either he will hate the one, and love the other; or else he will hold to the one, and despise the other. Ye cannot serve God and mammon. *Matt. 6:24*

No man, having put his hand to the plow, and looking back, is fit for the kingdom of God. *Luke 9:62*

To him that knoweth to do good, and doeth it not, to him it is sin. *Jas. 4:17*

INDUSTRY

Be thou diligent to know the state of thy flocks, and look well to thy herds. *Prov. 27:23*

He that tilleth his land shall have plenty of bread. *Prov. 28:19*

The ants are a people not strong, yet they prepare their meat in the summer. *Prov. 30:25*

INSTRUCTION

The fear of the Lord is the beginning of knowledge: but fools despise wisdom and instruction. *Prov. 1:7*

My son, hear the instruction of thy father, and forsake not the law of thy mother. *Prov. 1:8*

Train up a child in the way he should go: and when he is old, he will not depart from it. *Prov. 22:6*

JUDGMENT

Judge not, that ye be not judged. *Matt. 7:1*

With what judgment ye judge, ye shall be judged: and with what measure ye mete, it shall be measured to you again. *Matt. 7:2*

Why beholdest thou the mote that is in thy brother's eye, but considerest not the beam that is in thine own eye? *Matt. 7:3*

First cast out the beam out of thine own eye; and then shalt thou see clearly to cast out the mote out of thy brother's eye. *Matt. 7:5*

He that is without sin among you, let him first cast a stone. *John 8:7*

Woman, where are those thine accusers? hath no man condemned thee? *John 8:10*

KINDNESS

Inasmuch as ye have done it unto one of the least of these my brethren, ye have done it unto me. *Matt. 25:40*

As ye would that men should do to you, do ye also to them likewise. *Luke 6:31*

As we have therefore opportunity, let us do good unto all men. *Gal. 6:10*

LIFE

No man is sure of life. *Job 24:22*

Lord, make me to know mine end, and the measure of my days, what it is; that I may know how frail I am. *Psa. 39:4*

Seek the Lord, and ye shall live. *Amos 5:6*

He that loveth his life shall lose it. *John 12:25*

LOVE

Thou shalt love thy neighbour as thyself. *Lev. 19:18*

Thou shalt love the Lord thy God with all thine heart, and with all thy soul, and with all thy might. *Deut. 6:5*

Greater love hath no man than this, that a man lay down his life for his friends. *John 15:13*

We know that all things work together for good to them that love God. *Rom. 8:28*

If we love one another, God dwelleth in us, and his love is perfected in us. *1 John 4:12*

If a man say, I love God, and hateth his brother, he is a liar: for he that loveth not his brother whom he hath seen, how can he love God whom he hath not seen? *1 John 4:20*

MAN

God created man in his own image. *Gen. 1:27*

As for man, his days are as grass: as a flower of the field, so he flourisheth. *Psa. 103:15*

All are of the dust, and all turn to dust again. *Eccl. 3:20*

O Lord, thou art our Father; we are the clay, and thou our potter; and we all are the works of thy hand. *Isa. 64:8*

MARRIAGE

Therefore shall a man leave his father and his mother, and shall cleave unto his wife: and they shall be one flesh. *Gen. 2:23*

From the beginning of the creation God made them male and female. For this cause shall a man leave his father and mother, and cleave to his wife. *Mark 10:6, 7*

What therefore God hath joined together, let not man put asunder. *Mark 10:9*

Let the husband render unto the wife due benevolence: and likewise also the wife unto the husband. *1 Cor. 7:3*

MEEKNESS

The meek shall inherit the earth. *Psa. 37:11*

A soft answer turneth away wrath. *Prov. 15:1*

He that is slow to anger is better than the mighty: and he that ruleth his spirit than he that taketh a city. *Prov. 16:32*

Blessed are the meek: for they shall inherit the earth. *Matt. 5:5*

Whosoever shall smite thee on thy right cheek, turn to him the other also. *Matt. 5:39*

Take my yoke upon you, and learn of me; for I am meek and lowly in heart: and ye shall find rest unto your souls. *Matt. 11:29*

Bless them which persecute you: bless, and curse not. *Rom. 12:14*

If a man be overtaken in a fault, ye which are spiritual, restore such an one in the spirit of meekness; considering thyself, lest thou also be tempted. *Gal. 6:1*

MERCY

Like as a father pitieth his children, so the Lord pitieth them that fear him. *Psa. 103:13*

The mercy of the Lord is from everlasting to everlasting upon them that fear him. *Psa. 103:17*

Let not mercy and truth forsake thee: bind them about thy neck; write them upon the table of thine heart. *Prov. 3:3*

He that hath mercy on the poor, happy is he. *Prov. 14:21*

What doth the Lord require of thee, but to do justly, and to love mercy, and to walk humbly with thy God? *Mic. 6:8*

MINISTRY

Follow me, and I will make you fishers of men. *Matt. 4:18*

The harvest truly is great, but the labourers are few: pray ye therefore the Lord of the harvest, that he would send forth labourers into his harvest. *Luke 10:2*

How beautiful are the feet of them that preach the gospel of peace, and bring glad tidings of good things! *Rom. 10:15*

Feed the flock of God which is among you, taking the oversight thereof, not by constraint, but willingly; not for filthy lucre, but of a ready mind; Neither as being lords over God's heritage, but being examples to the flock. *1 Pet. 5:2, 3*

OBEY

Fear God, and keep his commandments: for this is the whole duty of man. *Eccl. 12:13*

If ye love me, keep my commandments. *John 14:15*

OPPORTUNITY

I must work the works of him that sent me, while it is day: the night cometh, when no man can work. *John 9:4*

Behold, now is the accepted time; behold, now is the day of salvation. *2 Cor. 6:2*

As we have therefore opportunity, let us do good unto all men. *Gal. 6:10*

PARENTS

Honour thy father and thy mother. *Ex. 10:12*

My son, hear the instruction of thy father, and forsake not the law of thy mother. *Prov. 1:8*

Whom the Lord loveth he correcteth; even as a father the son in whom he delighteth. *Prov. 3:12*

He that wasteth his father, and chaseth away his mother, is a son that causeth shame, and bringeth reproach. *Prov. 19:26*

Hearken unto thy father that begat thee, and despise not thy mother when she is old. *Prov. 23:22*

If a son shall ask bread of any of you that is a father, will ye give him a stone? *Luke 11:11*

Children, obey your parents in the Lord: for this is right. *Eph. 6:1*

PATIENCE

Those that wait upon the Lord, they shall inherit the earth. *Psa. 37:9*

My son, despise not the chastening of the Lord; neither be weary of his correction. *Prov. 3:11*

He that shall endure unto the end, the same shall be saved. *Matt. 24:13*

Now the God of patience and consolation grant you to be likeminded one toward another according to Christ Jesus. *Rom. 15:5*

The fruit of the Spirit is love, joy, peace, longsuffering, gentleness, goodness, faith. *Gal. 5:22*

Let us not be weary in well doing: for in due season we shall reap, if we faint not. *Gal. 6:9*

Put on . . . bowels of mercies, kindness, humbleness of mind, meekness, longsuffering; Forbearing one another, and forgiving one another. *Col. 3:12, 13*

Be patient toward all men. *1 Thess. 5:14*

PEACE AMONG MEN

Let there be no strife, I pray thee, between me and thee . . . for we be brethren. *Gen. 13:8*

The meek shall inherit the earth; and shall delight themselves in the abundance of peace. *Psa. 37:11*

He that is slow to anger is better than the mighty; and he that ruleth his spirit than he that taketh a city. *Prov. 16:32*

They shall beat their swords into plowshares, and their spears into pruninghooks. *Isa. 2:4*

Blessed are the peacemakers: for they shall be called the children of God. *Matt. 5:9*

Glory to God in the highest, and on earth peace, good will toward men. *Luke 2:14*

PEACE—SPIRITUAL

I will both lay me down in peace, and sleep: for thou, Lord, only makest me dwell in safety. *Psa. 4:8*

Peace I leave with you, my peace I give unto you: not as the world giveth, give I unto you. Let not your heart be troubled, neither let it be afraid. *John 14:27*

Being justified by Faith, we have peace with God through our Lord Jesus Christ. *Rom. 5:1*

The peace of God, which passeth all understanding, shall keep your hearts and minds through Christ Jesus. *Phil. 4:7*

Let the peace of God rule in your heart. *Col. 3:15*

PERFECTION

Let your heart therefore be perfect with the Lord our God, to walk in his statutes, and to keep his commandments. *1 Kin. 8:61*

Know thou the God of thy father, and serve him with a perfect heart and with a willing mind. *1 Chron. 28:9*

Be ye therefore perfect, even as your Father which is in heaven is perfect. *Matt. 5:48*

PERSECUTION

Blessed are they which are persecuted for righteousness' sake: for theirs is the kingdom of heaven. Blessed are ye, when men shall revile you, and persecute you, and shall say all manner of evil against you falsely, for my sake. Rejoice, and be exceeding glad: for great is your reward in heaven: for so persecuted they the prophets which were before you. *Matt. 5:10-12*

Love your enemies, bless them that curse you, do good to them that hate you, and pray for them which despitefully use you, and persecute you. *Matt. 5:44*

PESSIMISM

I looked on all the works that my hands had wrought, and on the labour that I had laboured to do: and, behold, all was vanity and vexation of spirit, and there was no profit under the sun. *Eccl. 2:11*

What profit hath he that hath laboured for the wind? *Eccl. 5:16*

There is not a just man upon earth, that doeth good, and sinneth not. *Eccl. 7:20*

PIETY

Blessed are they which do hunger and thirst after righteousness; for they shall be filled. *Matt. 5:6*

To love him with all the heart, and with all the understanding, and with all the soul, and with all the strength, and to love his neighbour as himself, is more than all whole burnt offerings and sacrifices. *Mark 12:33*

They that are after the flesh do mind the things of the flesh; but they that are after the Spirit the things of the Spirit. *Rom. 8:5*

PLENTY

Honour the Lord with thy substance . . . So shall thy barns be filled with plenty. *Prov. 3:9, 10*

The harvest truly is plenteous, but the labourers are few. *Matt. 9:37*

Give and it shall be given unto you; good measure, pressed down, and shaken together, and running over. *Luke 6:38*

POSSESSION

All things come of thee, and of thine own have we given thee. *1 Chron. 29:14*

Where your treasure is, there will your heart be also. *Matt. 6:21*

What is a man profited, if he shall gain the whole world, and lose his own soul? *Matt. 16:26*

A man's life consisteth not in the abundance of the things which he possesseth. *Luke 12:15*

Soul, thou hast much goods laid up for many years; take thine ease, eat, drink, and be merry. *Luke 12:19*

POVERTY

The needy shall not always be forgotten: the expectation of the poor shall not perish for ever. *Psa. 9:18*

A little that a righteous man hath is better than the riches of many wicked. *Psa. 37:16*

Wealth maketh many friends; but the poor is separated from his neighbour. *Prov. 19:4*

He that hath pity upon the poor lendeth unto the Lord; and that which he hath given will he pay him again. *Prov. 19:17*

PRAISE

I will praise the name of God with a song, and will magnify him with thanksgiving. *Psa. 69:30*

It is a good thing to give thanks unto the Lord, and to sing praises unto thy name, O most High. *Psa. 92:1*

Praise ye the Lord. O give thanks unto the Lord; for he is good: for his mercy endureth for ever. *Psa. 106:1*

PRAYER

Evening, and morning, and at noon, will I pray, and cry aloud: and he shall hear my voice. *Psa. 55:17*

In the day of my trouble I will call upon thee: for thou wilt answer me. *Psa. 86:7*

He will regard the prayer of the destitute, and not despise their prayer. *Psa. 102:17*

The Lord is nigh unto all them that call upon him, to all that call upon him in truth. *Psa. 145:18*

Seek ye the Lord while he may be found, call ye upon him while he is near. *Isa. 55:6*

Let us lift up our heart with our hands unto God in the heavens. *Lam. 3:41*

When thou prayest, thou shalt not be as the hypocrites are: for they love to pray standing in the synagogues and in the corners of the streets, that they may be seen of men. *Matt. 6:5*

When thou prayest, enter into thy closet, and when thou hast shut thy door, pray to thy Father which is in secret; and thy Father which seeth in secret shall reward thee openly. *Matt. 6:6*

Ask, and it shall be given you; seek, and ye shall find; knock, and it shall be opened unto you. *Matt. 7:7*

All things, whatsoever ye shall ask in prayer, believing, ye shall receive. *Matt. 21:22*

Whatsoever ye shall ask the Father in my name, he will give it you. *John 16:23*

Pray one for another. *Jas. 5:16*

PRIDE

Every one that is proud in heart is an abomination to the Lord. *Prov. 16:5*

Let not the wise man glory in his wisdom, neither let the mighty man glory in his might, let not the rich man glory in his riches: But let him that glorieth glory in this, that he understandeth and knoweth me, that I am the Lord which exercise lovingkindness, judgment, and righteousness, in the earth: for in these things I delight, saith the Lord. *Jer. 9:23, 24*

Whosoever will be great among you, let him be your minister; And whosoever will be chief among you, let him be your servant. *Matt. 20:26, 27*

Whoever shall exalt himself shall be abased; and he that shall humble himself shall be exalted. *Matt. 23:12*

REDEMPTION

The Son of man came not to be ministered unto, but to minister, and to give his life a ransom for many.
Matt. 20:28

This is my blood of the new testament, which is shed for many for the remission of sins. *Matt. 26:28*

I am the good shepherd: the good shepherd giveth his life for the sheep. *John 10:10*

There is one God, and one mediator between God and men, the man Christ Jesus; Who gave himself a ransom for all.
1 Tim. 5, 6

REGENERATION

Create in me a clean heart, O God; and renew a right spirit within me. *Psa. 51:10*

Except a man be born again, he cannot see the Kingdom of God. *John 3:3*

I am the light of the world: he that followeth me shall not walk in darkness, but shall have the light of life. *John 8:12*

I am come that they might have life, and that they might have it more abundantly. *John 10:10*

REJOICING

I will be glad and rejoice in thee: I will sing praise to thy name, O thou most High. *Psa. 9:2*

The Lord is my strength and my shield; my heart trusted in him, and I am helped: therefore my heart greatly rejoiceth; and with my song will I praise him. *Psa. 28:7*

REMORSE

The Lord is nigh unto them that are of a broken heart; and saveth such as be of a contrite spirit. *Psa. 34:18*

Have mercy upon me, O God, according to thy lovingkindness: according unto the multitude of thy tender mercies blot out my transgressions. *Psa. 51:1*

There shall be weeping and gnashing of teeth, when he shall see Abraham, and Isaac, and Jacob, and all the prophets, in the kingdom of God, and you yourselves thrust out.
Luke 13:28

I have sinned against heaven, and before thee, And am no more worthy to be called thy son. *Luke 15:18, 19*

REPENTANCE

If my people . . . shall humble themselves, and pray, and seek my face, and turn from their wicked ways; then will I hear from heaven, and will forgive their sin. *2 Chron. 7:14*

The Lord your God is gracious and merciful, and will not turn away his face from you, if ye return unto him.
2 Chron. 30:9

Except ye repent, ye shall all likewise perish. *Luke 13:3*

I will arise and go to my father, and will say unto him, Father, I have sinned against heaven, and before thee.
Luke 15:18

God be merciful to me a sinner. *Luke 18:13*

RESIGNATION

Be still, and know that I am God. *Psa. 46:10*

Teach me to do thy will; for thou art my God. *Psa. 143:10*

My son, despise not the chastening of the Lord; neither be weary of his correction. *Prov. 3:11*

If it be possible, let this cup pass from me: nevertheless not as I will, but as thou wilt. *Matt. 26:39*

RESPONSIBILITY

Am I my brother's keeper? *Gen. 4:9*

Every one of us shall give account of himself to God.
Rom. 14:12

Let us not therefore judge one another any more: but judge this rather, that no man put a stumblingblock or an occasion to fall in his brother's way. *Rom. 14:13*

RETALIATION

Whosoever shall smite thee on thy right cheek, turn to him the other also. *Matt. 5:39*

Avenge not yourselves, but rather give place unto wrath: for it is written, Vengeance is mine; I will repay, saith the Lord. *Rom. 12:19*

Not rendering evil for evil, or railing for railing: but contrariwise blessing. *1 Pet. 3:9*

REVERENCE

Ye shall keep my sabbaths, and reverence my sanctuary. *Lev. 19:30*

What doth the Lord thy God require of thee, but to fear the Lord thy God, to walk in all his ways, and to love him, and to serve the Lord thy God with all thy heart and with all thy soul. *Deut. 10:12*

Let all the earth fear the Lord: let all the inhabitants of the world stand in awe of him. *Psa. 33:8*

His salvation is nigh them that fear him. *Psa. 85:9*

REWARD

The Lord knoweth the days of the upright: and their inheritance shall be for ever. *Psa. 37:18*

The righteous shall inherit the earth. *Psa. 37:29*

Cast thy bread upon the waters: for thou shalt find it after many days. *Eccl. 11:1*

According to their deeds, accordingly he will repay. *Isa. 59:18*

Come, ye blessed of my Father, inherit the kingdom prepared for you from the foundation of the world: For I was an hungred, and ye gave me meat: I was thirsty, and ye gave me drink: I was a stranger, and ye took me in. *Matt. 25:34, 35*

Whosoever shall give you a cup of water to drink in my name . . . verily I say unto you, he shall not lose his reward. *Mark 9:41*

RIGHTEOUSNESS

Walk in the way of good men, and keep the paths of the righteous. *Prov. 2:20*

He that followeth after righteousness and mercy findeth life, righteousness, and honour. *Prov. 21:21*

SACRIFICE

The sacrifices of God are a broken heart. *Psa. 51:17*

If thou wilt be perfect, go and sell that thou hast, and give to the poor, and thou shalt have treasure in heaven: and come and follow me. *Matt. 19:20*

Present your bodies a living sacrifice, holy, acceptable unto God, which is your reasonable service. *Rom. 12:1*

SALVATION

Seek ye me, and ye shall live. *Amos 5:4*

Except ye be converted, and become as little children, ye shall not enter into the kingdom of God. *Matt. 18:3*

For God so loved the world, that he gave his only begotten Son, that whosoever believeth in him should not perish, but have everlasting life. *John 3:16*

He that heareth my word, and believeth on him that sent me, hath everlasting life, and shall not come into condemnation; but is passed from death unto life. *John 5:24*

I am the resurrection and the life: he that believeth in me, though he were dead, yet shall he live. *John 11:25*

Whosoever shall call upon the name of the Lord shall be saved. *Rom. 10:13*

SCRIPTURE

Seek ye out of the book of the Lord, and read. *Isa. 34:16*

Whosoever heareth these sayings of mine, and doeth them, I will liken him unto a wise man, which built his house upon a rock. *Matt. 7:24*

These are written, that ye might believe that Jesus is the Christ, the Son of God; and that believing ye might have life through his name. *John 20:31*

SELFISHNESS

Charity . . . seeketh not her own. *1 Cor. 13:4, 5*

Whoso hath this world's good, and seeth his brother have need, and shutteth up his bowels of compassion from him, how dwelleth the love of God in him? *1 John 3:17*

SELF-RIGHTEOUSNESS

Every way of a man is right in his own eyes: but the Lord pondereth the hearts. *Prov. 21:2*

God, I thank thee, that I am not as other men are. *Luke 18:9*

Let him that thinketh he standeth take heed lest he fall. *1 Cor. 10:12*

We should not trust in ourselves, but in God. *2 Cor. 1:9*

SIN

O God, thou knowest my foolishness; and my sins are not hid from thee. *Psa. 69:5*

As he thinketh in his heart, so is he. *Prov. 23:7*

All we like sheep have gone astray; we have turned every one to his own way. *Isa. 53:6*

Forgive us our sins. *Luke 11:4*

God be merciful to me a sinner. *Luke 18:13*

The wages of sin is death. *Rom. 6:23*

SLANDER

Deliver my soul, O Lord, from lying lips, and from a deceitful tongue. *Psa. 120:2*

Let all bitterness . . . and evil speaking, be put away from you, with all malice. *Eph. 4:31*

Speak evil of no man. *Tit. 3:2*

SORROW

He healeth the broken in heart, and bindeth up their wounds. *Psa. 147:3*

Surely he hath borne our griefs, and carried our sorrows. *Isa. 53:4*

Blessed are they that mourn: for they shall be comforted. *Matt. 5:4*

SPIRIT

Create in me a clean heart, O God; and renew a right spirit within me. *Psa. 51:10*

Then shall the dust return to the earth as it was: and the spirit shall return unto God who gave it. *Eccl. 12:7*

What shall it profit a man, if he shall gain the whole world, and lose his own soul? *Mark 8:36*

Flesh and blood cannot inherit the kingdom of God. *1 Cor. 15:50*

We know that if our earthly house of this tabernacle were dissolved, we have a building of God, an house not made with hands, eternal in the heavens. *2 Cor. 5:1*

STRENGTH

Be strong, and quit yourselves like men. *1 Sam. 4:9*

How are the mighty fallen! *2 Sam. 1:19*

The race is not to the swift, or the battle to the strong. *Eccl. 9:11*

They that wait on the Lord shall renew their strength; they shall mount up with wings as eagles; they shall run, and not be weary; and they shall walk, and not faint. *Isa. 40:31*

The Lord God is my strength. *Hab. 3:19*

SUFFERING

He was wounded for our transgressions, he was bruised for our iniquities. *Isa. 53:5*

I will shew him how great things he must suffer for my name's sake. *Acts 9:16*

Charity suffereth long. *1 Cor. 13:4*

If any man suffer as a Christian, let him not be ashamed; but let him glorify God on this behalf. *1 Pet. 4:16*

TEMPTATION

Whoso causeth the righteous to go astray in an evil way, he shall fall himself into his own pit. *Prov. 28:10*

Watch and pray, that ye enter not into temptation. *Matt. 26:41*

Let him that thinketh he standeth take heed lest he fall. *1 Cor. 10:12*

Resist the devil, and he will flee from you. *Jas. 4:7*

THANKSGIVING

O Lord my God, I will give thanks unto thee for ever. *Psa. 30:12*

It is a good thing to give thanks unto the Lord, and to sing praises unto thy name, O most High. *Psa. 92:1*

O give thanks unto the Lord, for he is good, for his mercy endureth for ever. *Psa. 107:1*

TOLERANCE

Why beholdest thou the mote that is in thy brother's eye, but considerest not the beam that is in thine own eye? *Matt. 7:3*

First cast out the beam out of thine own eye; and then shalt thou see clearly to cast out the mote out of thy brother's eye. *Matt. 7:5*

Speak evil of no man. *Tit. 3:2*

TROUBLE

The Lord also will be a refuge for the oppressed, a refuge in times of trouble. *Psa. 9:9*

God is our refuge and strength, a very present help in trouble. *Psa. 46:1*

Let not your heart be troubled: ye believe in God, believe also in me. *John 14:1*

TRUTH

I have chosen the way of truth. *Psa. 119:30*

Whatsoever things are true . . . think on these things. *Phil. 4:8*

UNBELIEF

The fool hath said in his heart, There is no God. *Psa. 14:1*

He that believeth and is baptized shall be saved; but he that believeth not shall be damned. *Mark 16:16*

O Jerusalem, Jerusalem, which killest the prophets, and stonest them that are sent unto thee; how often would I have fathered thy children together, as a hen doth gather her brood under her wings, and ye would not! *Luke 13:34*

He was in the world, and the world was made by him, and the world knew him not. *John 1:10*

He that believeth on the Son hath everlasting life: and he that believeth not the Son shall not see life; but the wrath of God abideth on him. *John 3:36*

UNSELFISHNESS

We then that are strong ought to bear the infirmities of the weak, and not to please ourselves. *Rom. 15:1*

I will very gladly spend and be spent for you. *2 Cor. 12:15*

VIGILANCE

Take ye heed, watch and pray: for ye know not when the time is. *Mark 13:33*

WAR

How are the mighty fallen in the midst of battle!
2 Sam. 1:25

The mighty . . . are gone down to hell with their weapons of war. *Ezek. 32:27*

All they that take the sword shall perish with the sword.
Matt. 26:52

Love your enemies. *Luke 6:27*

WEALTH

Beware that thou forget not the Lord thy God . . . when thou hast eaten and art full, and hast built goodly houses, and dwelt therein. *Deut. 8:11, 12*

He that trusteth in his riches shall fall. *Prov. 11:28*

Labour not to be rich. *Prov. 23:4*

Where your treasure is, there will your heart be also.
Matt. 6:21

It is easier for a camel to go through the eye of a needle, than for a rich man to enter into the kingdom of God.
Matt. 19:24

Ye cannot serve God and mammon. *Luke 16:13*

We brought nothing into this world, and it is certain we can carry nothing out. *1 Tim. 6:7*

WISDOM

Behold the fear of the Lord, that is wisdom; and to depart from evil is understanding. *Job 28:28*

The fear of the Lord is the beginning of wisdom: and the knowledge of the holy is understanding. *Prov. 9:10*

A man's wisdom maketh his face to shine. *Eccl. 8:1*

WORKS

Let your light so shine before men, that they may see your good works, and glorify your Father which is in heaven.
Matt. 5:16

Why call ye me, Lord, Lord, and do not the things which I say? *Luke 6:46*

Faith, if it hath not works, is dead. *Jas. 2:17*

WORSHIP

O come, let us worship and bow down: let us kneel before the Lord our maker. *Psa. 95:6*

I was glad when they said unto me, Let us go into the house of the Lord. *Psa. 122:1*

At the name of Jesus every knee should bow. *Phil. 2:10*

All nations shall come and worship before thee. *Rev. 15:4*

ZEAL

With my whole heart have I sought thee. *Psa. 119:10*

Let us not be weary in well doing: for in due season we shall reap, if we faint not. *Gal. 6:9*

CHAPTER VII

PRAYERS FOR VARIOUS OCCASIONS

IN THE MORNING AND IN THE EVENING

. . . Therefore it is well to let prayer be the first employment in the early morning and the last in the evening. Avoid diligently those false and deceptive thoughts which say, "wait a little, I will pray an hour hence; I must first perform this or that." For with such thoughts a man quits prayer for business, which lays hold of and entangles him so that he comes not to pray the whole day long. . . .

Martin Luther

THE LORD'S PRAYER

Our Father, who art in heaven, hallowed be thy Name. Thy kingdom come, Thy will be done, on earth as it is in heaven. Give us this day our daily bread. And forgive us our trespasses, as we forgive those who trespass against us. And lead us not into temptation, but deliver us from evil. For Thine is the kingdom, and the power, and the glory, for ever and ever. Amen.

PSALM 23

The Lord is my shepherd; I shall not want.

He maketh me to lie down in green pastures: he leadeth me beside the still waters.

He restoreth my soul; he leadeth me in the paths of righteousness, for his name's sake.

Yea, though I walk through the valley of the shadow of death, I will fear no evil; for thou art with me; thy rod and thy staff they comfort me.

Thou preparest a table before me in the presence of mine enemies: thou anointest my head with oil; my cup runneth over.

Surely goodness and mercy shall follow me all the days of my life: and I will dwell in the house of the Lord for ever.

CHILD'S MORNING PRAYER

Father, we thank Thee for the night,
And for the pleasant morning light;
For rest and food and loving care
And all that makes the world so fair.
Help us to do the things we should,
To be to others kind and good;
In all we do in work and play,
To love Thee better day by day.

Rebecca J. Weston

A CHILD'S EVENING PRAYER

Now I lay me down to sleep,
I pray the Lord my soul to keep;
If I should die before I wake,
I pray the Lord my soul to take.

EVENING PRAYER FOR A CHILD

Jesus, tender Shepherd, hear me;
  Bless Thy little lamb to-night;
Through the darkness be Thou near me;
  Keep me safe till morning light.

All this day Thy hand has led me,
  And I thank Thee for Thy care;
Thou hast warmed me, clothed and fed me;
  Listen to my evening prayer!

Let my sins be all forgiven;
  Bless the friends I love so well:
Take us all at last to heaven,
  Happy there with Thee to dwell.

Mary Duncan (*1839*)

A BIRTHDAY THOUGHT

I ask and wish not to appear
  More beauteous, rich or gay:

Lord, make me wiser every year,
And better every day.

Charles Lamb (1775-1834)

IN THE MORNING

O Lord, support us all the day long of this troublous life until the shadows lengthen and the evening comes, and the busy world is hushed, and the fever of life is over, and our work is done. Then in Thy mercy grant us a safe lodging and a holy rest, and peace at the last. Amen.

John Henry, Cardinal Newman (1801-1890)

WHO CAN TELL

Who can tell what a day may bring forth? Cause us, therefore, gracious God, to live every day as if it were to be our last, for that we know not but it may be such. Cause us to live so at present as we shall wish we had done when we come to die. O grant that we may not die with any guilt upon our consciences, or any known sin unrepented of, but that we may be found in Christ, Who is our only Saviour and Redeemer. Amen.

Thomas a. Kempis (1380-1471)

MAKE ME STRONGER

God, be patient with me, and make those who love me patient. Forgive, and help them to forgive, my weak resolve, my stubborn pride. Father, I know how I hurt Thee, and them, when I am unreasonable and demanding, when I lose my temper over trivial things. Make me stronger, O God; help me to keep the promises I make at night to Thee and to them to mend my ways on the morrow. Help me to be patient and forgiving with them as Thou art and they are with me. When I am in the wrong, give me the grace to admit it wholly, neither offering excuses nor trying to shift the blame. Make me more honest in my thinking, more charitable in my opinions.

Father, in Thy mercy Thou hast given me the love of family and friends; in Thy mercy help me to be worthy of it; for Thy dear Son's sake. Amen.

Anonymous

THAT WE MAY LOVE THEE

Almighty God, unto whom all hearts be open, all desires known, and from whom no secrets are hid; Cleanse the thoughts of our hearts by the inspiration of thy holy Spirit, that we may perfectly love thee, and worthily magnify thy holy Name; through Christ our Lord. Amen.

Bishop Leofric (1050)

HAVE MERCY UPON US

Almighty and most merciful Father; We have erred, and strayed from thy ways like lost sheep. We have followed too much the devices and desires of our own hearts. We have offended against thy holy laws. We have left undone those things which we ought to have done; And we have done those things which we ought not to have done; And there is no health in us. But thou, O Lord, have mercy upon us, miserable offenders. Spare thou those, O God, who confess their faults. Restore thou those who are penitent; According to thy promises declared unto mankind In Christ Jesus our Lord. And grant, O most merciful Father, for his sake; That we may hereafter live a godly, righteous, and sober life, To the glory of thy holy Name. Amen.

The Book of Common Prayer

A GRATEFUL HEART

Thou hast given so much to us, give one thing more, a grateful heart; for Christ's sake. Amen.

George Herbert (1593-1633)

FOR WORSHIP

O Almighty God, from Whom every good prayer cometh, and Who pourest out on all who desire it the spirit of grace and supplication, deliver us, when we draw nigh to Thee, from coldness of heart and wanderings of mind, that with steadfast thoughts and kindled affections we may worship Thee in spirit and in truth; through Jesus Christ our Lord. Amen.

William Bright (*1824-1901*)

THE DOXOLOGY

Praise God, from Whom all blessings flow!
Praise Him, all creatures here below!
Praise Him above, ye heavenly host!
Praise Father, Son, and Holy Ghost! Amen.

GUIDE AND GOVERN US

O Heavenly Father, in Whom we live and move and have our being, we humbly pray Thee so to guide and govern us by Thy Holy Spirit, that in all the cares and occupations of our daily life we may never forget Thee, but remember that we are ever walking in Thy sight; for Thine own Name's sake. Amen.

An Ancient Collect

PRIDE AND VANITY

Take from us, O God, all pride and vanity, all boasting and forwardness, and give us the true courage that shows itself by gentleness; the true wisdom that shows itself by simplicity; and the true power that shows itself by modesty; through Jesus Christ our Lord. Amen.

Charles Kingsley (*1819-1875*)

A CHILD'S GRACE

God is great and God is good,
And we thank Him for our food.
By His hand we all are fed.
Give us, Lord, our daily bread.
Amen.

A FAMILY GRACE

Bless, O Lord, this food to our use, and us to Thy service, and make us ever mindful of the needs of others. For Christ's sake. Amen.

NEW YEAR'S DAY

We ask Heaven's blessing to descend on the food which is before us. May this New Year find us more willing to do Thy bidding, for Christ's sake. Amen.

GRACE

Thou knowest, O Lord, what things we have need of before we ask Thee. All the blessings that we receive do constantly remind us of Thy unfailing love for us. We give Thee all praise. In Christ. Amen.

GRACE

O Lord, we thank Thee for life and the joy of living, for health and strength, and for these blessings fresh from Thine hand of love. Through Jesus Christ. Amen.

GRACE

Our Father, we bless Thee for this food and for all the expressions of Thy goodness to us. Give us grace to do Thy will, we pray through faith in Jesus Christ our Lord. Amen.

GRACE

Be present at our table, Lord;
Be here and everywhere adored.
These creatures bless, and grant that we
May feast in Paradise with Thee. Amen.

GRACE

Our Father we thank Thee for this food. Bless it to our good and give of Thy bounty to the poor and needy. We ask it in the name of our Saviour. Amen.

THANKSGIVING DAY

Once more we come, Lord, to the day of special thanksgiving. Our thoughts are turned backward. The days have rolled into the seasons, the seasons into the year. Each day has been crowded with Thee. Each season has brought forth new proofs of Thy loving forethought. May we this day pledge

Thee our gratitude anew. Continue, we pray Thee, to surround us with Thy care, in Jesus' name. Amen.

CHRISTMAS

We thank Thee for this day's feast, instituted by the Birth of Thy Holy Son. Bless us and guide us through all time, we ask for Jesus' sake. Amen.